James Elroy Flecker

To kathy
Thank you for your constant friendship
Love Linda

The Collected Poems of
James Elroy Flecker

Edited, with an Introduction,
by J. C. Squire

THIRTEENTH IMPRESSION

London
Martin Secker
Number Five John Street
Adelphi

First published	September 1916	1,000 Copies
Reprinted	September 1916	1,000 Copies
Reprinted	October 1916	1,000 Copies
Reprinted	January 1918	1,000 Copies
Reprinted	October 1919	1,000 Copies
Reprinted	June 1921	1,000 Copies
Reprinted	May 1922	1,000 Copies
Reprinted	April 1923	1,000 Copies
Reprinted	January 1924	1,000 Copies
Reprinted	October 1924	1,500 Copies
Reprinted	March 1926	1,500 Copies
Reprinted	November 1927	1,500 Copies
Reprinted	April 1929	1,500 Copies
		15,000

The frontispiece to this volume is from a
photograph of the Author taken
at Beyrout in 1912

LONDON : MARTIN SECKER (LTD.) 1929

Contents

vii

Introduction

I

JAMES ELROY FLECKER was born in London (Lewisham) on November 5, 1884. He was the eldest of the four children of the Rev. W. H. Flecker, D.D., now Head Master of Dean Close School, Cheltenham. After some years at his father's school he went in 1901 to Uppingham, proceeding to Trinity College, Oxford, in 1902. He stayed at Oxford until 1907 and then came to London, teaching for a short time in Mr. Simmons' school at Hampstead. In 1908 he decided to enter the Consular Service, and went up to Cambridge (Caius College) for the tuition in Oriental languages available there. He was sent to Constantinople in June 1910, was first taken ill there in August, and in September returned to England and went to a sanatorium in the Cotswolds. He returned to his post, apparently in perfect health, in March 1911; was transferred to Smyrna in April; and in May went on leave to Athens, where he married Miss Helle Skiadaressi, a Greek lady whom he had met in the preceding year. He spent three months' holiday in Corfu, and was sent to Beyrout, Syria, in September 1911. In December 1912 he took a month's leave in England and Paris, returning to Beyrout in January 1913. In March he again fell ill, and after a few weeks on the Lebanon (Brumana) he went to Switzerland, where, acting on his doctors' advice, he remained for the last eighteen months of his life. He stayed successively at Leysin, Montreux, Montana, Locarno, and (May 1914) Davos, where on January 3, 1915, he died. He is buried in Cheltenham at the foot of the Cotswold Hills.

His published books include :

Verse : " The Bridge of Fire " (Elkin Matthews, 1907), " Forty-two Poems " (Dent, 1911), " The Golden Journey to Samarkand " (Goschen, 1913, now published by Martin Secker), and " The Old Ships " (Poetry Bookshop, 1915).

Prose : " The Last Generation (New Age Press, 1908), " The Grecians " (Dent, 1910), " The Scholar's Italian Grammar " (D. Nutt, 1911), and " The King of Alsander " (Goschen, 1914, now published by Allen and Unwin). He left also two unpublished dramas, " Hassan " and " Don Juan," and a number of published and unpublished short stories, articles, and poems. Of the last all the most important will be found in the present volume.

II

That is the bare outline of Flecker's life and work. The present Introduction does not pretend to supply a " personal memoir," for which materials have not been collected ; and the work of estimating Flecker's art and " placing " him in relation to his contemporaries may be left to others. But one may usefully give a few more biographical details and a short analysis of the poet's artistic attitude and methods of work.

In person Flecker was tall, with blue eyes, black, straight hair, and dark complexion. There was a tinge of the East in his appearance, and his habitual expression was a curious blend of the sardonic and the gentle. Until illness incapacitated him he was physically quite active, but his principal amusement was conversation, of which he never tired. ◄ He felt acutely the loss of good talk during his years abroad, in Syria especially. He was sociable, and enjoyed meeting and talking with crowds of people; but he had few intimate friends at Oxford, and, after he left England, little opportunity of making any. One of the few, Mr. Frank Savery, now of the British Legation, Berne, sends the following notes:

"My acquaintance with him began in January 1901, when he was a lanky, precocious boy of sixteen, and lasted, with long interruptions, until his death. His fate took him to the Near East, mine took me to Germany: for this reason we never met from 1908 to 1914, though we never ceased to correspond. Largely because our intercourse was thus broken, I believe that I am better able to appreciate the changes which his character underwent in the latter years of his life than those who never lost sight of him for more than a few months at a time.

"It was at Oxford that I first came to know him intimately. He was extraordinarily undeveloped, even for an English Public School boy, when he first went up in 1902. He already wrote verses—with an appalling facility that for several years made me doubt his talent. He imitated with enthusiasm and without discrimination, and, the taste in those long-gone days being for Oscar Wilde's early verse and Swinburne's complacent swing, he turned out a good deal of decadent stuff, that was, I am convinced, not much better than the rubbish written by the rest of his generation at Oxford. What interested me in Flecker in those days was the strange contrast between the man—or rather the boy—and his work. Cultured Oxford in general, I should add, was not very productive at that time: a sonnet a month was about the maximum output of the lights of Balliol. The general style of literature in favour at the time did not lend itself to a generous outpouring. Hence there was a certain piquancy in the exuberant flow of passionate verse which issued from Flecker's ever-ready pen in spite of his entire innocence of any experience whatever.

" Furthermore, he was a wit—a great wit, I used to think, but no humorist—and, like most wits, he was combative. He talked best when some one baited him. At last it got to be quite the fashion in Oxford to ask Flecker to luncheon- and dinner-parties—simply in order to talk. The sport he afforded was usually excellent. . . . Looking back on it now, I believe I was right in thinking that in those days he had no humour (there is very little humour in Oxford) ; nor am I so entirely sure that his wit was bad. I had, at any rate, a growing feeling that, in spite of his immaturity and occasional bad taste, he was the most important of any of us : his immense productiveness was, I vaguely but rightly felt, better and more valuable than our finicky and sterile good taste.

" By 1906 he had developed greatly—largely thanks to the companionship of an Oxford friend whom, in spite of long absence and occasional estrangements, he loved deeply till the end of his life. Even his decadent poems had improved : poor as are most of the poems in ' The Bridge of Fire,' they are almost all above the level of

Oxford poetry, and there are occasional verses which forecast some of his mature work. Thus I still think that the title-poem itself is a rather remarkable achievement for a young man and not without a certain largeness of vision. The mention of this poem reminds me of an episode which well illustrates the light-heartedness which at that time distinguished the self-styled 'lean and swarthy poet of despair.' I was sitting with him and another friend in his rooms one day—early in 1906, I think—when he announced that he was going to publish a volume of poems. 'What shall I call it?' he asked. We had made many suggestions, mostly pointless, and almost all, I have no doubt, indecent, when Flecker suddenly exclaimed: 'I'll call it "The Bridge of Fire," and I'll write a poem with that name and put it in the middle of the book instead of the beginning. That'll be original and symbolic too.' We then debated the not unimportant question of what 'The Bridge of Fire' would be about. At midnight we parted, the question still unsettled. Flecker, however, remarked cheerfully that it did not much matter—it was a jolly good title and he'd easily be able to think of a poem to suit it.

"Flecker always cherished a great love for Oxford: he had loved it as an undergraduate, and afterwards not even the magic of the Greek seas, deeply as he felt it, ever made him forget his first university town. But on the whole I think that Cambridge, where he went to study Oriental languages in preparation for his consular career, did more for him. I only visited him once there—in November 1908, I think—but I had the distinct impression that he was more independent than he had been at Oxford. He was writing the first long version—that is to say, the third actual draft—of the 'King of Alsander.' Incidentally he had spoilt the tale, for the time being, by introducing a preposterous sentimental conclusion, a departure to unknown lands, if I remember rightly, with the peasant-maid, who had not yet been deposed, as she was later on, from her original position of heroine.

"And now follow the years in which my knowledge of Flecker is drawn only from a desultory correspondence. I should like to quote from some of the letters he wrote me, but, alas, they are in Munich with all my books and papers. He wrote to me at length whenever he had a big literary work on hand; otherwise an occasional post card sufficed, for he was a man who never put either news or gossip into his letters. I knew of his marriage; I knew that his literary judgment, as expressed in his letters and exemplified in his writings, had improved suddenly and phenomenally. That was all.

"At last his health finally collapsed and he came to Switzerland. It was at Locarno, in May 1914, that I saw him again. He was very ill, coughed continually, and did not, I think, ever go out during the whole fortnight I spent with him. He had matured even more than I had expected. . . .

"He was very cheerful that spring at Locarno—cheerful, not extravagantly optimistic, as is the way of consumptives. I think he hardly ever mentioned his illness to me, and there was certainly at that time nothing querulous about him. His judgment was very sound, not only on books but also on men. He confessed that he had not greatly liked the East—always excepting, of course, Greece —and that his intercourse with Mohammedans had led him to find more good in Christianity than he had previously suspected. I gathered that he had liked his work as Consul, and he once said to me that he was very proud

xiv

of having been a good businesslike official, thereby disposing, in his case at any rate, the time-honoured conception of the poet as an unpractical dreamer. He was certainly no mere dreamer at any period of his life; he appreciated beauty with extraordinary keenness, but, like a true poet, he was never contented with mere appreciation. He was determined to make his vision as clear to others as it was to himself.

"I saw Flecker once more, in December 1914. He was already visibly dying, and at times growing weakness numbed his faculties. But he was determined to do two things—to complete his poem, 'The Burial in England,' and to put his business affairs into the hands of a competent literary agent. The letters and memoranda on the latter subject which he dictated to me were admirably lucid, and I remember that, when I came to read them through afterwards, I found there was hardly a word which needed changing.

"One evening he went through the 'Burial' line by line with Mrs. Flecker and myself. He had always relied greatly on his wife's taste, and I may state with absolute certainty that the only two persons who ever really influenced him in literary matters were the Oxford friend I have already mentioned and the lady whose devotion prolonged his life, and whose acute feeling for literature helped to a great extent to confirm him in his lofty ideals of artistic perfection.

"Although he never really finished the longer version of the 'Burial' which he had projected, the alterations and additions he made that evening—'Toledo-wrought neither to break nor bend' was one of the latter—were in the main improvements and in no way suggested that his end was so near. To me, of course, that poem must always remain intolerably sad, but, as I re-read it the other day, I asked myself whether the casual reader would feel any trace of the 'mattrass grave' on which it was written. Candidly I do not think that even the sharpest of critics would have known, if he had not been told, that half the lines were written within a month of the author's death."

His letters, as is remarked above, were generally business-like and blunt. I have found a few to myself : they are almost all about his work, with here and there a short, exclamatory eulogy of some other writer. He observes, in December 1913, that a journal which had often published him had given "The Golden Journey" "an insolent ten-line review with a batch of nincompoops"; then alternately he is better and writing copiously, or very ill and not capable of a word. In one letter he talks of writing on Balkan Politics and Italy in Albania; in another of translating some war-poetry of Paul Deroulède's. Another time he is even thinking of "having a bang at the Cambridge Local Examination . . . with a whack in it at B. Shaw." Then in November 1914 he says : "I have exhausted myself writing heroic great war-poems." He might comprehensibly have been in low spirits, dying there in a dismal and deserted "health resort" among the Swiss mountains, with a continent of war-zones cutting him off from all chance of seeing friends. But he always wrote cheerfully, even when desperately ill. The French recovery filled him with enthusiasm; he watched the Near Eastern tangle with the peculiar interest of one who knew the peoples involved; and in one delicate and capricious piece of prose, published in a weekly in October, he recalled his own experiences of warfare. He had had glimpses of the Turco-Italian War : Italian shells over Beyrout (" Unforgettable the thunder of the guns shaking the golden blue of sky and sea while not a breath stirred the palm-trees, not a cloud moved on the swanlike snows of Lebanon ") and a " scrap " with the Druses, and the smoke and distant rumble of the battle of Lemnos, " the one effort of the Turks to secure the mastery of the Ægean." These were his exciting memories :

" To think that it was with cheerful anecdotes like these that I had hoped, a white-haired elder, to impress my grandchildren ! Now there's not a peasant from Picardy to Tobolsk but will cap me with tales of real and frightful tragedy. What a race of deep-eyed and thoughtful men we shall have in Europe—now that all those millions have been baptized in fire ! "

Then in the first week of January 1915 he died. I cannot help remembering that I first heard the news over the telephone, and that the voice which spoke was Rupert Brooke's.

III

Flecker began writing verse early, and one of his existing notebooks contains a number of poems written whilst he was at Uppingham. The original poems composed, at school and at Oxford, up to the age of twenty are not very remarkable. There is nothing unusual in some unpublished lines written on the school chapel bell at the end of his

last term, and little in " Danae's Cradle-Song for Perseus "
(1902).   A typical couplet is

Waste of the waves !   O for dawn !   For a long
   low level of shore !
Better be shattered and slain on the reef than
   drift evermore.

Both rhythm and language are Tennysonian, and the allite-
rative Tennysonianism at the end of the first line is repeated
in a " Song " of 1904 beginning :

Long low levels of land
   And sighing surges of sea,
Mountain and moor and strand
   Part my beloved from me.

A " Dream-Song " of 1904 is equally conventional, though
in the lines

Launch the galley, sailors bold,
Prowed with silver, sharp and cold,
Winged with silk and oared with gold,

may be seen the first ineffective attempt to capture an
image that in various forms haunted Flecker to the end
of his life.   But the most numerous and, on the whole,
the best of his early poems are translations.   And this is
perhaps significant, as indicating that he began by being
more interested in his art than in himself.   Translating,
there was a clearly defined problem to be attacked ; diffi-
culties of expression could not be evaded by changing the
thing to be expressed ; and there was no scope for fluent
reminiscence or a docile pursuit at the heels of the rhyme.

In 1900–1, *æt.* 16–17, he was translating Catullus and the "Pervigilium Veneris," and amongst the poets he attacked in the next few years were Propertius, Muretus, Heine, Bierbaum, of whose lyrics he translated several, one of which is given in this volume. This habit of translation, so excellent as a discipline, he always continued, amongst the poets from whom he made versions being Meleager, Goethe, Leconte de Lisle, Baudelaire, H. de Régnier, Samain, Jean Moréas, and Paul Fort. In the last year or two his translations were mostly made from the French Parnassians. What drew him to them was his feeling of especial kinship with them and his belief that they might be a healthy influence on English verse.

He explained his position in the preface to "The Golden Journey to Samarkand." The theory of the Parnassians had for him, he said, "a unique attraction." "A careful study of this theory, however old-fashioned it may by now have become in France, would, I am convinced, benefit English critics and poets, for both our poetic criticism and our poetry are in chaos." Good poetry had been written on other theories and on no theories at all, and "no worthless writer will be redeemed by the excellence of the poetic theory he may chance to hold." But "that a sound theory can produce sound practice and exercise a beneficent effect on writers of genius" had been repeatedly proved in the history of the Parnasse.

"The Parnassian School [he continued] was a classical reaction against the perfervid sentimentality and extravagance of some French Romantics. The Romantics in France, as in England, had done their powerful work and infinitely widened the scope and enriched the language of poetry. It remained for the Parnassians to raise the technique of their art to a height which should enable them to express the subtlest ideas in powerful and simple verse. ● But the real meaning of the term Parnassian may be best understood from considering what is definitely not Parnassian. To be didactic like Wordsworth, to write dull poems of unwieldy length, to bury like Tennyson or Browning poetry of exquisite beauty in monstrous realms of vulgar, feeble, or obscure versifying, to overlay fine work with gross and irrelevant egoism like Victor Hugo, would be abhorrent, and rightly so, to members of this school. On the other hand, the finest work of many great English poets, especially Milton, Keats, Matthew Arnold, and Tennyson, is written in the same tradition as the work of the great French school : and one can but wish that the two latter poets had had something of a definite theory to guide them in self-criticism. Tennyson would never have published ' Locksley Hall ' and Arnold might have refrained from spoiling his finest sonnets by astonishing cacophonies."

There were, he naturally admitted, "many splendid forms of passionate or individual poetry " which were not Parnassian, such as the work of Villon, Browning, Shelley, Rossetti, and Verlaine, " too emotional, individual, or eccentric " to have Parnassian affinities :

" The French Parnassian has a tendency to use traditional forms and even to employ classical subjects. *His desire in writing poetry is to create beauty: his inclination is toward a beauty somewhat statuesque. He is apt to be dramatic and objective rather than intimate.* The enemies

of the Parnassians have accused them of cultivating unemo-
tional frigidity and upholding an austere view of perfection.
The unanswerable answers to all criticism are the works of
Hérédia, Leconte de Lisle, Samain, Henri de Régnier, and
Jean Moréas. Compare the early works of the latter poet,
written under the influence of the Symbolists, with his
' Stances ' if you would see what excellence of theory can
do when it has genius to work on. Read the works of
Hérédia, if you would understand how conscious and
perfect artistry, far from stifling inspiration, fashions it
into shapes of unimaginable beauty. . . . At the present
moment there can be no doubt that English poetry stands
in need of some such saving doctrine to redeem it from the
formlessness and the didactic tendencies which are now in
fashion. As for English criticism, can it not learn from
the Parnassian, or any tolerable theory of poetic art, to
examine the beauty and not the ' message ' of poetry."

" It is not [he said] the poet's business to save man's
soul but to make it worth saving. . . . However, few poets
have written with a clear theory of art for art's sake, it
is by that theory alone that their work has been, or can
be, judged ;—and rightly so if we remember that art
embraces all life and all humanity, and sees in the tem-
porary and fleeting doctrines of conservative or revolu-
tionary only the human grandeur or passion that inspires
them."

His own volume had been written " with the single inten-
tion of creating beauty."

Though many of his own poems show the " tendency to
use traditional forms and even to employ classical subjects,"
Flecker did not, it must be observed, dogmatize as to

choice of subject or generalize too widely. The Parnassians were not everything to him, nor were those older poets who had resembled them. It was as a corrective that he recommended the study of this particular group to his English contemporaries. It is arguable that most of his major contemporaries—one might instance Mr. Bridges and Mr. Yeats—are anything but chaotic, extravagant, careless, or didactic. References to " the latest writer of manly tales in verse " and " formlessness " might certainly be followed up ; but formlessness and moralizing are not so universal amongst modern English writers as Flecker, making out his case, implied. It does not matter ; there is not even any necessity to discuss the French Parnassians. Flecker had an affinity with them. He disliked the pedestrian and the wild ; he did not care either to pile up dramatic horrors or to burrow in the recesses of his own psychological or physiological structure. He liked the image, vivid, definite in its outline : he aimed everywhere at clarity and compactness. His most fantastic visions are solid and highly coloured and have hard edges. His imagination rioted in images, but he kept it severely under restraint, lest the tropical creepers should stifle the trees. Only occasionally, in his later poems, a reader may find the language a little tumultuous and the images heaped so profusely as to produce an effect of obscurity and, sometimes, of euphuism. But these poems, it must be remembered, are precisely those which the poet himself did not finally revise. Some of them he never even finished : " The Burial in England," as it appears, is the best that can be done with a confusing collection of manuscript thoughts and second thoughts. He was, as he claimed, constitutionally a classic; but the term must not be employed too rigidly. He was, in fact, like Flaubert, both a classic and a romantic. He combined, like Flaubert, a romantic taste for the exotic, the gorgeous, and the violent, with a dislike for the romantic egoism, looseness of structure, and turgidity of phrase. His objectivity, in spite of all his colour, was often very marked; but there was another trend in him. Though he never wrote slack and reasonless *vers libres*, the more he developed the more he experimented with new rhythms; and one of his latest and best lyrics was the intensely personal poem " Stillness." He ran no special kind of subject too hard, and had no refined and restricted dictionary of words. A careful reader, of course, may discover that there are words, just as there are images, which he was especially fond of using. There are colours and metals, blue and red, silver and gold, which are present everywhere in his work; the progresses of the sun (he was always a poet of the sunlight rather than a poet of the moonlight) were a continual fascination to him; the images of Fire, of a ship, and of an old white-bearded man recur frequently in his poems. But he is anything but a monotonous poet, in respect either of forms, subjects, or language. It was characteristic of him that he should be on his guard against falling into a customary jargon. Revising " The Welsh Sea " and finding the word " golden," which he felt he and others had overdone, used three times (and not ineffectively) in it, he expunged the adjective outright, putting " yellow " in the first two places and " slow green " in the third. His preface on

Parnassianism was whole-hearted ; but any one who interpreted some of his sentences as implying a desire to restrict either the poet's field or his expression to a degree that might justifiably be termed narrow would be in error. In one respect, perhaps, his plea was a plea for widening ; he did not wish to *exclude* the classical subject. And his declaration that poetry should not be written to carry a message but to embody a perception of beauty did not preclude a message in the poetry. His last poems, including " The Burial in England," may be restrained but are scarcely impersonal, may not be didactic but are none the less patriotic. He need not, in fact, be pinned to every word of his preface separately. The drift of the whole is evident. He himself, like other people, would not have been where he was but for the Romantic movement ; but he thought that English verse was in danger of decomposition. He merely desired to emphasize the dangers both of prosing and of personal paroxysms ; and, above all, to insist upon careful craftsmanship.

This careful craftsmanship had been his own aim from the beginning. " Libellum arida modo pumice expolitum " is a phrase in the first of the Catullus epigrams he translated at school ; and, whilst the content of his poetry showed a steadily growing strength of passion and thought, its form was subjected to, though it never too obviously " betrayed," an increasingly assiduous application of pumice-stone and file. His poems were written and rewritten before they were printed ; some were completely remodelled after their first publication ; and he was continually returning to his old poems to make alterations in single words or lines—many of his recent MS. alterations are now incorporated for the first time. His changes at their most extensive may be seen in the development of " The Bridge of Fire," in that (both versions are given in this volume) of " Narcissus," and in that of " Tenebris Interlucentem." As first published this ran :

> Once a poor song-bird that had lost her way
> Sang down in hell upon a blackened bough,
> Till all the lazy ghosts remembered how
> The forest trees stood up against the day.
>
> Then suddenly they knew that they had died,
> Hearing this music mock their shadow-land ;
> And some one there stole forth a timid hand
> To draw a phantom brother to his side.

In the second version, also of eight lines, each line is shorter by two syllables :

> A linnet who had lost her way
> Sang on a blackened bough in Hell,
> Till all the ghosts remembered well
> The trees, the wind, the golden day.
>
> At last they knew that they had died
> When they heard music in that land,
> And some one there stole forth a hand
> To draw a brother to his side.

The details of this drastic improvement are worth studying. The treatment of the first line is typical. The general word " song-bird " goes, the particular word "linnet" is substituted; and the superfluous adjective is cut out, like several subsequent ones. "Gravis Dulcis Immutabilis" was originally written as a sonnet; the "Invitation to a Young but Learned Friend" was considerably lengthened after an interval of years; and the poet's own copies of his printed volumes are promiscuously marked with minor alterations and re-alterations. One of the most curious is that by which the sexes are transposed in the song printed first as "The Golden Head" and then as "The Queen's Song." The last four lines of the first stanza originally ran:

> I then might touch thy face
> Delightful Maid,
> And leave a metal grace,
> A graven head.

This was altered into:

> I then might touch thy face
> Delightful boy,
> And leave a metal grace,
> A graven joy.

The reasons for the alteration are evident. The sounds "ace" and "aid" are uncomfortably like each other; the long, lingering "oy" makes a much better ending of the stanza than the sound for which it was substituted; and the false parallelism of "metal grace" and "graven head" was remedied by eliminating the concrete word and replacing it by another abstract one on the same plane as "grace." Such a substitution of the abstract for the concrete word, sound enough here, is very rare with him;

normally the changes were the other way round. He preferred the exact word to the vague ; he was always on his guard against the " pot-shot " and the complaisant epithet which will fit in anywhere. With passionate deliberation he clarified and crystallized his thoughts and intensified his pictures.

He found, as has been said, kinship in the French Parnassians : and, though he approached them rather as a comrade than as a disciple, traces of their language, especially perhaps that of de Régnier and Hérédia, may be found in his later verse. A reading of Hérédia is surely evident in the " Gates of Damascus " : in

Beyond the towns, an isle where, bound, a naked giant
    bites the ground :
The shadow of a monstrous wing looms on his back :
    and still no sound.

and the stanzas surrounding it. An influence still more marked is that of Sir Richard Burton. Flecker, when still a boy, had copied out the whole of his long " Kasidah," and its rhythms and turns of phrase are present in several of his Syrian poems. It was in the " Kasidah " that Flecker found Aflatun and Aristu, and the refrain of " the tinkling of the camel-bells " of which he made such fine use in " The Golden Journey." The verse-form of the " Kasidah " is, of course, not Burton's, it is Eastern ; and the use Flecker made of it suggests that an infusion of Persian and Arabic forms into English verse might well be a fertilizing agent. He always read a great deal of Latin verse : Latin poetry was as much to him as Greek history, myth, and landscape. Francis Thompson, Baudelaire, and Swinburne were all early "influences." He learnt from them but he was seldom mastered by them. He did not imitate their rhythms or borrow their thought. The Swinburnian "Anapæsts"—in the first volume—written in a weak moment, were an exception. In Flecker's printed copy the title has first, in a half-hearted effort to save the poem whilst repudiating its second-hand music and insincere sentiments, been changed to "Decadent Poem"; and then a thick pencil has been drawn right through it. From his English contemporaries Flecker was detached. He admired some of them—Mr. Yeats, Mr. A. E. Housman, Mr. de la Mare, and others; and with some he was friendly, especially Rupert Brooke, with whom he had been at Cambridge. Of Mr. Chesterton's "Flying Inn" he writes in January 1914: "A magnificent book—his masterpiece; and the humorous verse splendid." But his physical absence, first in the Levant and then in Switzerland, in itself prevented him from getting into any literary set, and his temperament and opinion of current tendencies was such that, even had he lived in England, he would probably have escaped "infection" by any school or individual. Flecker's vision of the world was his own; his dreams of the East and Greece were born with him. He knew the streets of Stamboul and the snows of Lebanon, and the caravans departing for Bagdad and the gates of Damascus, and the bazaars heaped with grapes and "coffee-tables botched with pearl and little beaten brassware pots"; but his hankering long antedated his travels. There is an unpublished poem written when he was twenty

in which voices call him " to white Ægean isles among the
foam " and the " dreamy painted lands " of the East. In
the same year he translated Propertius I, xx. His life-
long love of Greek names is shown by his enunciation of
them even then :

> But Oreithyia's sons have left him now :
> Hylas, most foolish boy, where goest thou ?
> He is going to the Hamadryades,
> To them devoted—I will tell you how.
>
> There's a clear well beneath Arganthos' screes
> Wherein Bithynian Naiads take their ease,
> By leafage overarched, where apples hide
> Whilst the dew kisses them on the unknown trees.

This poem is dated 1904. It is the year of the Glion
stanzas, the sonnet on Francis Thompson, and (probably)
the fragmentary " Ode on Shelley." It is the year, that
is, when Flecker began to show marks of maturity. The
translation, like a number of other early poems quoted
above, has not been included in the present collection,
as it is certain that Flecker would not have wished it.
Just enough of his unpublished " Juvenilia " have been
included to illustrate his development, and it may be
alleged without rashness that those selected are the best
of their respective periods.

Whatever may be said about the poems which follow,
there are few which are not characteristic of the poet.
His rigorous conception of his art and his fidelity to his
own vision prevented many lapses, and he suppressed
those which he did commit. One unrepresentative phrase

there is which might be seized on to give a very untrue description of him. In the Envoy to "The Bridge of Fire" he speaks of himself as "the lean and swarthy poet of despair." It meant nothing; the first poem in the same book, with its proclamation that "the most surprising songs" must still be sung, and its challenge to youth to turn to "the old and fervent goddess" whose eyes are "the silent pools of Light and Truth" is far more characteristic of him, first and last. "Lean and swarthy poet" may stand; but not of despair. The beauty of the world was a continual intoxication to him; he was full, as a man, if not as a poet, of enthusiasms, moral and material, economic, educational, and military. Neither the real nor the spurious disease of pessimism is present in his verse and in his last autumn he was writing, with an energy that sometimes physically exhausted him, poems that blazed with courage, hope, and delight. Like his "Old Battleship," he went down fighting.

The value of what he has left it is not, as I have said before, my intention to discuss here. My only object in writing this necessarily rather disjointed Introduction is to give some information that may interest the reader and be useful to the critic; and if a few personal opinions have slipped in they may conveniently be ignored. A vehement "puff preliminary" is an insolence in a volume of this kind: it might pardonably be supposed to imply either doubts about the author or distrust of his readers.

J. C. SQUIRE

Editorial Note

*Twenty of the poems in this edition have never been published
before, or have appeared only in periodicals. These may be
distinguished by the dates which are appended beneath them.
The whole of the poems published in book form during the
poet's lifetime are reprinted with the exception of seven lyrics
which there is reason to believe he did not desire to perpetuate.
Of the new ones several are "Juvenilia," written between the
ages of sixteen and twenty, which have been included in order
to illustrate his development.*

*The poems are arranged in a roughly chronological order ;
those written in the years 1907–10 following most nearly
(more information as to date being available with these) the
actual order of composition.*

*The text of many, especially of the early, poems will be
found to differ considerably from that hitherto printed, owing
to Flecker's habit of continual revision. In some of the
MSS. there are variant readings from which the present
editor has been compelled to select. The fragments of the
"Ode to Shelley" presented the most difficult problem, and
the order in which they are placed is not to be presumed the
correct order.*

JUVENILIA

Four Translations and Adaptations
from Catullus

I

For whom this pretty pamphlet, polished new
With pumice-stone ?   Cornelius, for you :
For you were never unprepared to deem
My simple verses worthy of esteem,
Though you yourself—who else in Rome so bold ?—
In volumes three have laboured to unfold
A " Universal History of Man "—
Dear Jove !   A learnèd and laborious plan !

Wherefore to you, my friend, I dedicate
This so indifferent bookling ; yet I pray,
Poor as it is—O goddess of my fate,
Let it outlive the writer's transient day !

1900 (?) : *æt.* 16

III

Cupids and loves, and men of gentler mien,
Mourn, for my lady's lovèd one is dead,
Her darling sparrow that to her hath been
Dearer than her own eyes : even as a maid
Loveth her mother, so had he been bred
To know his mistress. He was honeysweet
Nor ever truant from her bosom strayed,
But there would twitter from his soft retreat.
And now—he's flitting down the Shadow Way,
Ah, never to return ! A curse on ye,
Black shades of death, that let no fair thing stay ;
How fair a sparrow have ye snatched from me !

Poor birdie—all for thee the teardrops rise,
Till red with weeping are my Love's bright eyes.

1900

IV

Proud is Phaselus here, my friends, to tell
That once she was the swiftest craft afloat :
No vessel, were she winged with blade or sail,
Could ever pass my boat.

4

Phaselus shunned to shun grim Adria's shore,
Or Cyclades, or Rhodes the wide renowned,
Or Bosphorus, where Thracian waters roar,
Or Pontus' eddying sound.
It was in Pontus once, unwrought, she stood,
And conversed, sighing, with her sister trees,
Amastris born, or where Cytorus' wood
Answers the mountain breeze.
Pontic Amastris, boxwood-clad Cytorus !—
You, says Phaselus, are her closest kin :
Yours were the forests where she stood inglorious :
The waters yours wherein
She dipped her virgin blades ; and from your strand
She bore her master through the cringing straits,
Nought caring were the wind on either hand,
Or whether kindly fates
Filled both the straining sheets.   Never a prayer
For her was offered to the gods of haven,
Till last she left the sea, hither to fare,
And to be lightly laven
By the cool ripple of the clear lagoon.

     .   .   .   .   .

This too is past ; at length she is allowed
Long slumber through her life's long afternoon,
To Castor and the twin of Castor vowed.

1901

X

When lounging idle mid forensic whirl,
Friend Varus took me off to see his girl.
The naughty wench, I very soon was shewn,
Had got some wit and beauty of her own.
Arriving, we began a busy chat
On politics, and weather, this and that—
Then on my province's internal state,
And " Had I found the profit adequate ? "
I answered truthfully, " There's nothing there
For common soldier or for officer
Wherewith to purchase grease for home-bound hair."
" You found at least "—said she—" one always can :
Some aboriginals for your sedan ? "
Said I in answer, posing for her eyes
In prosperous and fashionable guise,
" Oh, really, I was not so penniless
That any mere provincial distress
Should render me incompetent to get
Eight smartish bearers for the voiturette."
(In truth there was no slave in all the earth
Whom I could then have summoned to my hearth
To shoulder the debilitated leg
Of my old pallet.)   " Then, dear friend, I beg "—
Cries she most aptly for so bad a minx—
" I want to pay a visit to the Sphinx—
You'll lend them me just to the temple door,
My sweet Catullus ? "

              " Oh, you may be sure "—
Said I—" I would—but what I mentioned now
As mine—I just forgot—what matter how ?—
My messmate Cinna, Gaius Cinna, he
Has commandeered them. Really, as for me,
What difference if you call them his or mine ?
I use them just whenever I incline.
But you're a silly pestilential jade
To want a chance remark so nicely weighed."

                                 1901

Sirmio

Little gem of all-but-islands and of islands, Sirmio,
Whether set in landlocked waters, or in Ocean's freer flow—
Oh the pleasant seeing of thee, bright as ever—there below—
Far behind me, to the Northward, lie the dreamy lands
of snow.
Oh the hour of mad rejoicing, oh the sweet good-bye to woe
As with quiet soul aweary of world-wandering to and fro
In we hurry through the doorway of our home of long
ago. . . .
Hail then, hail! Thy master welcome, welcome him,
sweet Sirmio,
Leap for joy, ye tumbling waters, winking at the summer's
glow,
Gaily through the house resounding let the peals of laughter
go.

1901–04

Lucretia

As one who in the cold abyss of night
Stares at a book whose grey print meaningless
Dances between the lamplight and his eyes,
Lucretius lay, soul-poisoned, conquering still
With towering travail Reason's Hellene heights.
Listen, Lucretia, to the voice of his pain :

Thrice welcome hour of Reason : ne'er of old
Knew I thy naked loveliness, till night,
The nether night of Folly pinioned forth,
Shrouded my senses, taught me terribly
That thou alone, my light and life and love,
Wearest the high insignia of the stars.
Grant then thy worshipper, austerest Queen,
Refreshing dews—Now, now, I thirst with flame :
They flee the strainings of my fevered lips
Cruelly, and in dank distance a new noise
Of rushing wings I hear.   Who thunders nigh ?
Devil delirium, chaos charioted,
Curb, curb, the coal-red chargers, heard not seen
See, Madam Wife, that loveless lust of thine

Leaves no sweet savour lingering, but a curse :
And 'stead of Love and Reason, palace tenant,
There flits a weak and tremulous loathsomeness !

Suppliant fled Lucretia to the couch :
And all her glory trembled as she sang :

Awake, dead soul of dear Lucretius,
Awake, thy witless fond destroyer prays.
Awake, awake, and quit thy aimless journey
In old oblivion's purple-misted paths.
   Dost thou remember, husband ?   It was evening :
We wandered shorewards, mid the ocean of air
That glassed the gliding Nereids of the Pole.
Immeasurable moonlight kissed the brow
Of the white sea whose ripples swayed to greet
Our heart's unnumbered laughter.   Strongest sleep
So held the life of earth that dimly we heard
Time's fatal pulse through the dark reverberated.
Then died thy soul : that night I, murderess, dreamt,
Ah, dolorous dreams of limb-dissolving love.
Lucretius,
Why live I still, protracting hopeless pain ?
The chillness of the long Lethean stream
Is more to be commended for my sailings
Than love's hot eddies.
                              God, for the draught of death !
What sourer, sweeter vintage could be pressed ?

10

To slumber shall I lull me, where no sorrow
Can pierce the drifted overmantling haze:
No sorrow, no despair, nor any love!

My soul is thine, husband, thy mad soul.
Madness, swift foretaste of oblivion
Shall wed us to delirious dim despair
Till bone claim bone beneath the cypress tree.
What pleasant dawn of madness! Off I rend
This fair hypocrisy of raiment. Down—
There's fairer guile within—down, frippery!
Veil me not from my love. Dear arms outstretched,
Am I not fair? These quick white limbs of mine
Shall brand in thee their passionate symmetry,
Till as the bee within the lily trembles
Thyself, body and soul, shall move within me.
Has sculptured Venus thighs of richer vein?
Spread thyself round about me; let us wrench
Self unto self. Why life is lovely still!
Fair wings of madness, drift us far away
To an unseen Empyrean, where no care
Can frost the magic mirror of our loves.
Thence we shall see the sorrowful world of men,
Old castles fired, old mountains overturned,
Old majesties conculcate in the dust,
With short sad smiles for every thing destroyed.
Why do red eyes draw nearer? Husband, wake!
The palace is fired and falling! Not with love
Thy body's life, that throbs within me, burns

11

Lucretius—those same eyes, grey Furies wear them,
They seethe in double dullness 'neath their own!

Thus muttered she in dread : he glaring lay :
Passion had made him beast, and passion sated
Did leave him than the beasts more bestial.
Till phantomed reason fled his turning brain
And with a cry he struck her from his breast,
Heavily, and her hair, like the finger of night,
Pencilled the marble as she fell, and cried :

Kill me not, devil : off, blood-searching hands ;
Nay, strike me thus—and rend me thus, and thus :
I would not be the mother of mad children.
Burst forth, my blood, burst forth from wound and weal.
The body's pain is blister for the soul's.

Then, as her anguish slumbered for awhile :

Oh for a word of consolation dear
Sadder than dirge from old Simonides,
Sweeter than echoes of the Linos song
Whispering through the drowsy sheaves of corn
On summer evenings, when the harvesters
Homeward return, and children rush to greet
Their father, and to snatch the kisses first—

But a new torment rent her, and she rose ;
Her veins large-knotted, standing out in fire ;
She grasped his arm and shrieked to the solemn sun
That rolled in horror down the Western Sea :

There, red-eyed Fury—with lash and terrible hiss,
With lash and terrible hiss of steaming snakes—
Blood from the breast-wound drips, and from my heart,
And from those eyes, and from the pillars—See
There, and the statues move. Take away the blank eyes !
  Oh wild, wild irony of Life and Lust,
Life is to death so near, and lust to loathing.
All is a jest, a shadow, and a lie.
A whirlwind-wondrous lie !
                    Laugh, husband, laugh !
Laughter is man's supreme prerogative :
The beasts are sane ; they laugh not. I will laugh,
My bones and flesh are quaking. Laugh, thou fool !
For love is lust, and life is a dream of death
—Hell is opening, opening horribly.

March 1904

Song in the Night

(*From Bierbaum*)

Streets to left, and streets to right,
  Dull and dank it seems,
As I wander in the night
  Wakened from my dreams.
      Yearning,
      Burning,
    Pain and smart,
Whither dost thou sink, my heart ?
Whither dost thou sink, my heart ?

There's a house with shutters green
  Far away from town,
Where the river rolls serene
  Moving, murmuring down.
      Bowers,
      Flowers !
    Fold it in !
Would I were a guest within !
Would I were a guest within !

June 1904

14

Glion—Noon

From Glion on an August noon
  I scarcely see the ripples shine
Where sunbeam spirits lightly swoon
  On drifting shrouds of cyanine.

The Dent du Midi now uprears
  His proud tiara through the mist,
The sacred crown whose triple tiers
  Are walls of Titan amethyst.

A voiceless, dreamless paradise
  Of fleeting and fantastic form
More lovely than the fierce sunrise,
  More visionary than the storm.

Here would I dream away long years
  Till with the mountains I was one,
Knowing not loves or hates or fears,
  Standing immutably alone.

15

Glion—Evening

From Glion when the sun declines
   The world below is clear to see :
I count the escalading pines
   Upon the rocks of Meillerie.

Like a dull bee the steamer plies
   And settles on the jutting pier :
The barques, strange sailing butterflies,
   Round idle headlands idly veer.

The painted sceneries recall
   Such toil as Canaletto spent
To give each brick upon each wall
   Its due partition of cement.

Yet rather seem those lands below
   From Glion at the close of day
As vivid as a cameo
   Graved by the poet Gautier.

July 1904

Last Love

(From Novalis—adaptation of his last words)

Now for a last glad look upon life : my journey is ending :
Now this door that is Death quietly shuts me behind.
Thankful I hear Love's call—the faithful call of a comrade :
Then all joyful am I, ready to give her my heart.
All through life it is Love hath been my counsellor only :
Hers be the praise alway if I have followed aright.
For as a mother awakes with kisses her slumbering baby,
As she first has a care—as she alone understands—
So has Love been mine, has watched and tended and kissed
    me :
Near me when I was a child : near me till I was a man.
Thus, mid sorrow or doubt, I have clung to her, learning
    her lesson :
Now she has made me free—free to rejoice evermore.

1904 ?

Fragments of an Ode to Shelley

I

Since men have always crowned the tomb
With those sweet diadems of doom,
The twinings of memorial flowers,
So that their brother's first few hours
Of waiting in his lonely room
May pass in peace while Time devours
The body's brief and bitter bloom,
The last extortion of sad powers,
And downwards through the grudging soil
The piteous perfumes strain and toil,

II

Let the kind ritual remain :
We seek an emblem of our pain—
The dry scant holly of the shore,
The grass upon the dunes—What more
Can sorrow bring ? We cannot drain

The spacious Sea for his rich store
Of coloured weeds that shine in vain
Upon the wide inhuman floor,
The lonely yard where drowned men lie
And gaze through water to white sky.

III

Forgive, thou calm and godlike shade,
The drooping wreath, the flowers that fade,
This passionless pale offering
From one who scarcely dares to sing
His love and praises, being afraid
At the sweet brilliance of thy spring,
Seeing his lute is rudely made,
His thoughts too dull and weak of wing,
More fit for noons that lull and warm
Than for the stress of fire and storm.

IV

The slender boat that stretched her sail
To fly before the sultry gale,
That from her moorings leapt and sped
Before the forest leaves were red,
Before the purple noon was pale,

Round whom delight and fancy spread
Their guardian wings, without avail,
Is shipwrecked, and her captain dead.
The children of the stainless sea
Laid him ashore mysteriously.

V

O none of those who came to mourn
The body cold and water-worn,
Nor any of us in later days
Who walk at evening in soft ways
Could bring thee tribute of the morn
Or any music that repays
The soul of Adonais, borne
To heaven on thy fluted phrase.
Poets have wept ; but which of them
Were fit to sing thy requiem ?

VI

That song shall wait till delving time
Finds the lost treasures of earth's prime,
When moil and tears and dire distress
Shall flee the dawn of joyousness,
When some new monarch of sweet rhyme

Or mild surprising poetess,
Some Sappho in a mood sublime
Or Pindar freed and fetterless,
In a far island in far seas
Shall send their sorrow down the breeze.

*　　*　　*

O shining servant of the evening star
Whom no soft footfall of Lethean song
Delighted, but a strong celestial war
To batter down the gates of earthly wrong,
To thee old Rhea yielded up her foison,
Thou rash knight-errant of heroic love,
That dreams and trances, being most vital poison
To whoso looks but dares not live above,
For thee, who wast more bold,
Might lead to earth along light chains of gold,
Lest some rebellious airs of spirit
Should blow each image into windy space
Nor leave it vocal, to inherit
The toil and triumph of our mortal race.
O thou hast shown us legions in the skies,
And passed the earth before us in review
Till shadows came and went before our eyes,
And shafts of dim desire pierced us through,
　　　And draughts of joyous day
　　　And winds that calmly blew
Swift strength and splendour in our dreams, and songs
　　from far away.

*　　*　　*

Light and the subtler light of wizard fire,
And winds that strike forth hope on some grand lyre,
And spirits of blue air like April clouds,
And all the water-company that crowds
The river-spaces and dark open sea,
Conspired at his creation : Liberty,
Watching his prowess from her tower above,
Took to her side a royal-wingèd Love.
And when he died and they could do no more
To strengthen him who graced that southern shore
They bade a clearer, stronger sun arise
And drive old darkness from the Italian skies.

*   *   *

Many there be to-day whose foolish praise
Has dulled the roar of thy old fighting days,
So that thy hymns of intellectual joy
Seem but fine utterance of a wayward boy,
Thy call of war, thy thunderbolts of hate
A madman's cry, that rails against his fate ;
Who find in them a vague and phantom truth
Or dim ideal of a lovelorn youth.

*   *   *

He was too beautiful ; he died too young,
Before the mellow season of his prime ;
Sweet songs he left, but sweeter songs unsung,
Whose thin ghosts wander out of space and time.
All his philosophy was Love and Hate,
His life a rainbow for the sun to fashion,
His thoughts most royally importunate,

Forged by the beats of elemental passion.
Like some young tressèd tree
That sighs to each . . . wind, so he
Stretched arms to welcome Love, who softly winging
Came down to earth from lands beyond the dawn ;
Her strength and gentleness inspired his singing,
Until she stood amazed, from whom 'twas drawn.
Spirit of love, draw near this monument
And veil the ancient glory of thy head,
For he is dead, whose silver days were spent
In thy eternal service, he is dead
        And borne aloft away
        On gloomy wings outspread
More strong and sure than thy bright plumes,
        O mistress of a day !

       *   *   *

[EPODE]

Nothing of him is left us, save this scroll,
The fire-thrown shadow of his silent soul,
The glass whose even rondure is to keep
The immortal country of his mortal sleep.
Where terrors move and angry phantoms cry,
Titans and tyrants in a ragged sky,
Where in tall caves magicians read the rune,
And white limbs glitter in the plenilune ;

And where a voice more human, more divine,
Commends a brother dead to Proserpine
But now that Queen of undivided rest
Reopening the closures of her breast
Has taken our royal-wingèd child of light,
And bathed his forehead in the pool of night.

[Date uncertain, early]

LATER POEMS

A New Year's Carol

Awake, awake ! The world is young,
For all its weary years of thought :
The starkest fights must still be fought,
The most surprising songs be sung.

And those who have no other Gods
May still behold, if they bestir,
The windy amphitheatre
Where dawn the timeless periods.

Then hear the shouting-voice of men
Magniloquently rise and ring :
Their flashing eyes and measured swing
Prove that the world is young again.

I was beyond the hills, and heard
That old and fervent Goddess call,
Whose voice is like a waterfall,
And sweeter than the singing-bird.

27

O stubborn arms of rosy youth,
Break down your other Gods, and turn
To where her dauntless eyeballs burn,—
The silent pools of Light and Truth.

From Grenoble

Now have I seen, in Graisivaudan's vale,
The fruits that dangle and the vines that trail,
The poplars standing up in bright blue air,
The silver turmoil of the broad Isère
And sheer pale cliffs that wait through Earth's long noon
Till the round Sun be colder than the Moon.

Mine be the ancient song of Travellers :
I hate this glittering land where nothing stirs :
I would go back, for I would see again
Mountains less vast, a less abundant plain,
The Northern Cliffs clean-swept with driven foam,
And the rose-garden of my gracious home.

Narcissus

O thou with whom I dallied
  Through all the hours of noon,—
Sweet water-boy, more pallid
  Than any watery moon ;
Above thy body turning
  White lily-buds were strewn :
Alas, the silver morning,
  Alas, the golden noon !

Alas, the clouds of sorrow,
  The waters of despair !
I sought thee on the morrow,
  And never found thee there.
Since first I saw thee splendid,
  Since last I called thee fair,
My happy ways have ended
  By waters of despair.

The pool that was thy dwelling
  I hardly knew again,
So black it was, and swelling
  With bitter wind and rain.

Amid the reeds I lingered
  Between desire and pain
Till evening, rosy-fingered,
  Beckoned to night again.

Yet once when sudden quiet
  Had visited the skies,
And stilled the stormy riot,
  I looked upon thine eyes.
I saw they wept and trembled
  With glittering mysteries,
But yellow clouds assembled
  Redarkening the skies.

O listless thou art lying
  In waters cool and sweet,
While I, dumb brother, dying,
  Faint in the desert heat.
Though thou dost love another,
  Still let my lips entreat :
Men call me fair, O brother,
  And women honey-sweet.

Inscription for Arthur Rackham's
Rip Van Winkle

Since youth is wise, and cannot comprehend
Proportion, nor behold things as they are,
Φιλοθεάμονες we'll be, my friend,
And laugh at what appears quadrangular.
Our only Gods shall be the Subterrane,
Pictures of things misshapen, harsh and crude,
The flattened Face outside the window-pane,
The little Squeak behind us in the wood.
Here, friend, are subtly drawn uncommon things :
Make such your Gods : they only understand.
Only a Headless Ape with slimy wings
Can whisk you round the Interesting Land.
Though after twenty years they may not please,
Sane men have worshipped stranger Gods than these.

Envoy

The young men leap, and toss their golden hair,
Run round the land, or sail across the seas :
But one was stricken with a sore disease,—
The lean and swarthy poet of despair.

Know me, the slave of fear and death and shame,
A sad Comedian, a most tragic Fool,
Shallow, imperfect, fashioned without rule,
The doubtful shadow of a demon flame.

Rioupéroux

High and solemn mountains guard Rioupéroux,
—Small untidy village where the river drives a mill :
Frail as wood anemones, white and frail were you,
And drooping a little, like the slender daffodil.

Oh I will go to France again, and tramp the valley through,
And I will change these gentle clothes for clog and corduroy,
And work with the mill-hands of black Rioupéroux,
And walk with you, and talk with you, like any other boy.

Mignon

(From Goethe)

Knowest thou the land where bloom the lemon trees,
And darkly gleam the golden oranges ?
A gentle wind blows down from that blue sky ;
Calm stands the myrtle and the laurel high.
Knowest thou the land ?   So far and fair !
Thou, whom I love, and I will wander there.

Knowest thou the house with all its rooms aglow,
And shining hall and columned portico ?
The marble statues stand and look at me.
Alas, poor child, what have they done to thee ?
Knowest thou the land ?   So far and fair.
My Guardian, thou and I will wander there.

Knowest thou the mountain with its bridge of cloud i
The mule plods warily : the white mists crowd.
Coiled in their caves the brood of dragons sleep ;
The torrent hurls the rock from steep to steep.
Knowest thou the land ?   So far and fair.
Father, away !   Our road is over there !

Tenebris Interlucentem

A linnet who had lost her way
Sang on a blackened bough in Hell,
Till all the ghosts remembered well
The trees, the wind, the golden day.

At last they knew that they had died
When they heard music in that land,
And some one there stole forth a hand
To draw a brother to his side.

The First Sonnet of Bathrolaire

Over the moonless land of Bathrolaire
Rises at night, when revelry begins,
A white unreal orb, a sun that spins,
A sun that watches with a sullen stare
That dance spasmodic they are dancing there,
Whilst drone and cry and drone of violins
Hint at the sweetness of forgotten sins,
Or call the devotees of shame to prayer.
And all the spaces of the midnight town
Ring with appeal and sorrowful abuse.
There some most lonely are : some try to crown
Mad lovers with sad boughs ot formal yews
And Titan women wandering up and down
Lead on the pale fanatics of the muse.

The Second Sonnet of Bathrolaire

Now the sweet Dawn on brighter fields afar
Has walked among the daisies, and has breathed
The glory of the mountain winds, and sheathed
The stubborn sword of Night's last-shining star.
In Bathrolaire when Day's old doors unbar
The motley mask, fantastically wreathed,
Pass through a strong portcullis brazen teethed,
And enter glowing mines of cinnabar.
Stupendous prisons shut them out from day,
Gratings and caves and rayless catacombs,
And the unrelenting rack and tourniquet
Grind death in cells where jetting gaslight gloams,
And iron ladders stretching far away
Dive to the depths of those eternal domes.

The Ballad of Hampstead Heath

From Heaven's Gate to Hampstead Heath
  Young Bacchus and his crew
Came tumbling down, and o'er the town
  Their bursting trumpets blew.

The silver night was wildly bright,
  And madly shone the Moon
To hear a song so clear and strong,
  With such a lovely tune.

From London's houses, huts and flats,
  Came busmen, snobs, and Earls,
And ugly men in bowler hats
  With charming little girls.

Sir Moses came with eyes of flame,
  Judd, who is like a bloater,
The brave Lord Mayor in coach and pair,
  King Edward, in his motor.

Far in a rosy mist withdrawn
The God and all his crew,
Silenus pulled by nymphs, a faun,
A satyr drenched in dew,

Smiled as they wept those shining tears
Only Immortals know,
Whose feet are set among the stars,
Above the shifting snow.

And one spake out into the night,
Before they left for ever,
" Rejoice, rejoice ! " and his great voice
Rolled like a splendid river.

He spake in Greek, which Britons speak
Seldom, and circumspectly ;
But Mr. Judd, that man of mud,
Translated it correctly.

And when they heard that happy word,
Policemen leapt and ambled :
The busmen pranced, the maidens danced,
The men in bowlers gambolled.

A wistful Echo stayed behind
To join the mortal dances,
But Mr. Judd, with words unkind,
Rejected her advances.

And passing down through London Town
  She stopped, for all was lonely,
Attracted by a big brass plate
  Inscribed, FOR MEMBERS ONLY.

And so she went to Parliament,
  But those ungainly men
Woke up from sleep, and turned about,
  And fell asleep again.

Litany to Satan

(*From Baudelaire*)

O grandest of the Angels, and most wise,
O fallen God, fate-driven from the skies,
Satan, at last take pity on our pain.

O first of exiles who endurest wrong,
Yet growest, in thy hatred, still more strong,
Satan, at last take pity on our pain !

O subterranean King, omniscient,
Healer of man's immortal discontent,
Satan, at last take pity on our pain.

To lepers and to outcasts thou dost show
That Passion is the Paradise below.
Satan, at last take pity on our pain.

Thou by thy mistress Death hast given to man
Hope, the imperishable courtesan.
Satan, at last take pity on our pain.

Thou givest to the Guilty their calm mien
Which damns the crowd around the guillotine
Satan, at last take pity on our pain.

Thou knowest the corners of the jealous Earth
Where God has hidden jewels of great worth.
Satan, at last take pity on our pain.

Thou dost discover by mysterious signs
Where sleep the buried people of the mines.
Satan, at last take pity on our pain.

Thou stretchest forth a saving hand to keep
Such men as roam upon the roofs in sleep.
Satan, at last take pity on our pain.

Thy power can make the halting Drunkard's feet
Avoid the peril of the surging street.
Satan, at last take pity on our pain.

Thou, to console our helplessness, didst plot
The cunning use of powder and of shot.
Satan, at last take pity on our pain.

Thy awful name is written as with pitch
On the unrelenting foreheads of the rich.
Satan, at last take pity on our pain.

In strange and hidden places thou dost move
Where women cry for torture in their love.
Satan, at last take pity on our pain.

Father of those whom God's tempestuous ire
Has flung from Paradise with sword and fire,
Satan, at last take pity on our pain.

PRAYER

Satan, to thee be praise upon the Height
Where thou wast king of old, and in the night
Of Hell, where thou dost dream on silently.
Grant that one day beneath the Knowledge-tree
When it shoots forth to grace thy royal brow,
My soul may sit, that cries upon thee now.

44

The Translator and the Children

While I translated Baudelaire,
Children were playing out in the air.
Turning to watch, I saw the light
That made their clothes and faces bright.
I heard the tune they meant to sing
As they kept dancing in a ring ;
But I could not forget my book,
And thought of men whose faces shook
When babies passed them with a look.

They are as terrible as death,
Those children in the road beneath.
Their witless chatter is more dread
Than voices in a madman's head :
Their dance more awful and inspired,
Because their feet are never tired,
Than silent revel with soft sound
Of pipes, on consecrated ground,
When all the ghosts go round and round.

Destroyer of Ships, Men, Cities

Helen of Troy has sprung from Hell
   To claim her ancient throne,
So we have bidden friends farewell
   To follow her alone.

The Lady of the laurelled brow,
   The Queen of pride and power,
Looks rather like a phantom now,
   And rather like a flower.

Deep in her eyes the lamp of night
   Burns with a secret flame,
Where shadows pass that have no sight,
   And ghosts that have no name.

For mute is battle's brazen horn
   That rang for Priest and King,
And she who drank of that brave morn
   Is pale with evening.

An hour there is when bright words flow,
  A little hour for sleep,
An hour between, when lights are low,
  And then she seems to weep.

But no less lovely than of old
  She shines, and almost hears
The horns that blew in days of gold,
  The shouting charioteers.

And she still breaks the hearts of men,
  Their hearts and all their pride,
Doomed to be cruel once again,
  And live dissatisfied.

Oxford Canal

When you have wearied of the valiant spires of this
County Town,
Of its wide white streets and glistening museums, and
black monastic walls,
Of its red motors and lumbering trams, and self-sufficient
people,
I will take you walking with me to a place you have
not seen—
Half town and half country—the land of the Canal.
It is dearer to me than the antique town : I love it
more than the rounded hills :
Straightest, sublimest of rivers is the long Canal.
I have observed great storms and trembled : I have
wept for fear of the dark.
But nothing makes me so afraid as the clear water of
this idle canal on a summer's noon.
Do you see the great telephone poles down in the water,
how every wire is distinct ?
If a body fell into the canal it would rest entangled in
those wires for ever, between earth and air.
For the water is as deep as the stars are high.

48

One day I was thinking how if a man fell from that
lofty pole
He would rush through the water toward me till his
image was scattered by his splash,
When suddenly a train rushed by : the brazen dome of
the engine flashed : the long white carriages roared ;
The sun veiled himself for a moment, and the signals
loomed in fog ;
A savage woman screamed at me from a barge : little
children began to cry ;
The untidy landscape rose to life ; a sawmill started ;
A cart rattled down to the wharf, and workmen clanged
over the iron footbridge ;
A beautiful old man nodded from the first story window
of a square red house,
And a pretty girl came out to hang up clothes in a
small delightful garden.
O strange motion in the suburb of a county town : slow
regular movement of the dance of death !
Men and not phantoms are these that move in light.
Forgotten they live, and forgotten die.

Hialmar Speaks to the Raven

(*From Leconte de Lisle*)

Night on the bloodstained snow : the wind is chill :
And there a thousand tombless warriors lie,
Grasping their swords, wild-featured. All are still.
Above them the black ravens wheel and cry.

A brilliant moon sends her cold light abroad :
Hialmar arises from the reddened slain,
Heavily leaning on his broken sword,
And bleeding from his side the battle-rain.

" Hail to you all : is there one breath still drawn
Among those fierce and fearless lads who played
So merrily, and sang as sweet in the dawn
As thrushes singing in the bramble shade ?

" They have no word to say : my helm's unbound,
My breastplate by the axe unriveted :
Blood's on my eyes ; I hear a spreading sound,
Like waves or wolves that clamour in my head.

" Eater of men, old raven, come this way,
And with thine iron bill open my breast,
To-morrow find us where we lie to-day,
And bear my heart to her that I love best.

" Through Upsála, where drink the Jarls and sing,
And clash their golden bowls in company,
Bird of the moor, carry on tireless wing
To Ylmer's daughter there the heart of me.

" And thou shalt see her standing straight and pale,
High pedestalled on some rook-haunted tower :
She has two ear-rings, silver and vermeil,
And eyes like stars that shine in sunset hour.

" Tell her my love, thou dark bird ominous ;
Give her my heart, no bloodless heart and vile
But red compact and strong, O raven. Thus
Shall Ylmer's daughter greet thee with a smile.

" Now let my life from twenty deep wounds flow,
And wolves may drink the blood. My time is done.
Young, brave and spotless, I rejoice to go
And sit where all the Gods are, in the sun."

The Ballad of the Student in the South

It was no sooner than this morn
   That first I found you there,
Deep in a field of southern corn
   The colour of your hair.

I had read books you had not read,
   Yet I was put to shame
To hear the simple words you said,
   And see your eyes aflame.

Shall I forget when prying dawn
   Sends me about my way,
The careless stars, the quiet lawn,
   And you with whom I lay ?

Yours is the beauty of the moon,
   The wisdom of the sea,
Since first you tasted, sweet and soon,
   Of God's forbidden tree.

Darling, a scholar's fancies sink
  So faint beneath your song;
And you are right, why should we think,
  We who are young and strong?

For we are simple, you and I,
  We do what others do,
Who live because they fear to die
  And love the whole night through.

The Queen's Song

Had I the power
    To Midas given of old
To touch a flower
    And leave the petals gold
I then might touch thy face,
    Delightful boy,
And leave a metal grace,
    A graven joy.

Thus would I slay,—
    Ah, desperate device!
The vital day
    That trembles in thine eyes,
And let the red lips close
    Which sang so well,
And drive away the rose
    To leave a shell.

Then I myself,
    Rising austere and dumb
On the high shelf
    Of my half-lighted room,

Would place the shining bust
       And wait alone,
Until I was but dust,
       Buried unknown.

Thus in my love
       For nations yet unborn,
I would remove
       From our two lives the morn,
And muse on loveliness
       In mine arm-chair,
Content should Time confess
       How sweet you were.

On Turner's Polyphemus

Painter of day, let my dark spirit fly
  Past the Trinacrian Sound, to gaze upon
  The deathless horses of Hyperion
Driven up fiery stairs tumultuously :
To see once more the Achaian prows glide by,
  Odysseus in his burnished galleon,
  Nereides that sing him swiftly on,
And baffled Cyclops fading in the sky.

Master, you paint the passion of the Earth,
The faint victorious music of her birth,
  The splendour of things lost and things grown old ;
And show us song new-wrought with ardent might
Of strong-winged morning and of sure delight,
  Of hyacinthine mist, and shining gold.

The Bridge of Fire

I

High on the bridge of Heaven whose Eastern bars
Exclude the interchange of Night and Day,
Robed with faint seas and crowned with quiet stars
All great Gods dwell to whom men prayed or pray.
No winter chills, no fear or fever mars
Their grand and timeless hours of pomp and play;
Some drive about the Rim wind-golden cars
Or, shouting, laugh Eternity away.
  The daughters of their pride,
  Moon-pale, blue-water-eyed,
Their flame-white bodies pearled with failing spray,
  Send all their dark hair streaming
  Down where the worlds lie gleaming,
And draw their mighty lovers close and say :
  " Come over by the Stream : one hears
The speech of Nations broken in the chant of Spheres."

II

Hear now the song of those bright Shapes that shine
Huge as Leviathans, tasting the fare
Delicate-sweet, while scented dews divine
Thrill from the ground and clasp the rosy air,
" Sing on, sing out, and reach a hand for wine,
For the brown small Earth is softly afloat down there,
And the suns burn low, and the sky is sapphirine,
And the little winds of space are in our hair—
  The little winds of space
  Blow in the love-god's face,
The only god who lacks not praise and prayer ;
  He shall preserve his powers
  Though Ruin shake square towers
And echoing Temples fall without repair,
  And still go forth as strong as ten,
A red immortal riding in the hearts of men ! "

III

The Gods whose faces are the morning light
Of they who love the leafy rood of song,
The Gods of Greece, dividing the broad night,
Have gathered on the Bridge, of all that throng
The fairest, whether he whose feet for flight
Had plumy wings, or she to whom belong
Shadows, Persephone, or that swan-white

Rose-breasted island lady, gentle and strong,
　　Or younger gods than these
　　That peep among the trees
And dance when Dionysus beats his gong,
　　Or the old disastrous gods
　　That nod with snaky nods
Brandishing high the sharp and triple thong,
　　Or whom the dull profound of Hell
Spits forth, the reeling Typhon that in dark must dwell.

IV

Shadows there are that seem to look for home
Each spreading like a gloom across the plain,
Voiced like a great bell swinging in a dome,
Appealing mightily for realms to reign.
They were the slow and shapeless gods of Rome,
Laborious gods, who founded power on pain,
These watched the peasant turn his sullen loam,
These drave him out to fight, nor drave in vain :
　　Saturnus white and old
　　Who lost the age of gold,
Mars who was proud to stand on the deep-piled slain,
　　Pomona from whose womb
　　Slow fruits in season come,
And, tower-crowned mother of the yellow grain,
　　Demeter, and the avenging dead,
The silent Lemures, in fear with honey fed.

59

V

Belus and Ra and that most jealous Lord
Who rolled the hosts of Pharaoh in the sea,
Trolls of the North, in every hand a sword,
Gnomes and dwarfs and the shuddering company,
Gods who take vengeance, gods who grant reward,
Gods who exact a murdered devotee,
Brahma the kind, and Siva the abhorred
And they who tend Ygdrasil, the big tree,
  And Isis, the young moon,
  And she of the piping tune,
Her Phrygian sister, cruel Cybele,
  Orpheus the lone harp-player
  And Mithras the man-slayer,
And Allah rumbling on to victory,
  And some, the oldest of them all,
Square heads that leer and lust, and lizard shapes that
  crawl.

VI

Between the pedestals of Night and Morning,
Between red death and radiant desire
With not one sound of triumph or of warning
Stands the great sentry on the Bridge of Fire.
O transient soul, thy thought with dreams adorning,
Cast down the laurel, and unstring the lyre :

The wheels of Time are turning, turning, turning,
The slow stream channels deep and doth not tire.
 Gods on their Bridge above
 Whispering lies and love
Shall mock your passage down the sunless river
 Which, rolling all its streams,
 Shall take you, king of dreams,
—Unthroned and unapproachable for ever—
 To where the kings who dreamed of old
Whiten in habitations monumental cold.

We That Were Friends

We that were friends to-night have found
   A fear, a secret, and a shame :
I am on fire with that soft sound
   You make, in uttering my name.

Forgive a young and boastful man
   Whom dreams delight and passions please,
And love me as great women can
   Who have no children at their knees.

My Friend

I had a friend who battled for the truth
With stubborn heart and obstinate despair,
Till all his beauty left him, and his youth,
And there were few to love him anywhere.

Then would he wander out among the graves,
And think of dead men lying in a row ;
Or, standing on a cliff, observe the waves,
And hear the wistful sound of winds below ;

And yet they told him nothing.   So he sought
The twittering forest at the break of day,
Or on fantastic mountains shaped a thought
As lofty and impenitent as they.

And next he went in wonder through a town
Slowly by day and hurriedly by night,
And watched men walking up the street and down
With timorous and terrible delight.

Weary, he drew man's wisdom from a book,
And pondered on the high words spoken of old,
Pacing a lamplit room : but soon forsook
The golden sentences that left him cold.

After, a woman found him, and his head
Lay on her breast, till he forgot his pain
In gentle kisses on a midnight bed,
And welcomed royal-winged joy again.

When love became a loathing, as it must,
He knew not where to turn ; and he was wise,
Being now old, to sink among the dust,
And rest his rebel heart, and close his eyes.

Ideal

When all my gentle friends had gone
I wandered in the night alone :
Beneath the green electric glare
I saw men pass with hearts of stone.
Yet still I heard them everywhere,
Those golden voices of the air :
" Friend, we will go to hell with thee,
Thy griefs, thy glories we will share,
And rule the earth, and bind the sea,
And set ten thousand devils free ;—"
" What dost thou, stranger, at my side,
Thou gaunt old man accosting me ?
Away, this is my night of pride !
On lunar seas my boat will glide
And I shall know the secret things."
The old man answered : " Woe betide ! "
Said I : " The world was made for kings :
To him who works and working sings
Come joy and majesty and power
And steadfast love with royal wings."
" O watch these fools that blink and cower,"
Said that wise man : " and every hour

65

A score is born, a dozen dies."
Said I : " In London fades the flower;
But far away the bright blue skies
Shall watch my solemn walls arise,
And all the glory, all the grace
Of earth shall gather there, and eyes
Will shine like stars in that new place."
Said he : " Indeed of ancient race
Thou comest, with thy hollow scheme.
But sail, O architect of dream,
To lands beyond the Ocean stream.
Where are the islands of the blest,
And where Atlantis, where Theleme ? "

Mary Magdalen

O eyes that strip the souls of men!
There came to me the Magdalen.
Her blue robe with a cord was bound,
Her hair with knotted ivy crowned.
" Arise," she said, " God calls for thee,
Turned to new paths thy feet must be.
Leave the fever and the feast,
Leave the friend thou lovest best :
For thou must walk in barefoot ways,
On hills where God is near to praise."

Then answered I—" Sweet Magdalen,
God's servant, once beloved of men,
Why didst thou change old ways for new,
Thy trailing red for corded blue,
The rose for ivy on thy brow,
That splendour for this barren vow ? "
Gentle of speech she answered me :—
" Sir, I was sick with revelry.
True, I have scarred the night with sin,
A pale and tawdry heroine ;

Yet once I heard a voice that said,
' Who lives in sin is like one dead,
But follow : thy dark eyes shall see
The towns of immortality.' "

" O Mary, not for this," I cried,
" Didst thou renounce thy scented pride
Not for the roll of endless years
Or fields of joy undewed by tears
Didst thou desert the courts of men.
Tell me thy truth, grave Magdalen ! "

She trembled, and her eyes grew dim :—
" For love of Him, for love of Him."

I Rose from Dreamless Hours

I rose from dreamless hours and sought the morn
That beat upon my window : from the sill
I watched sweet lands, where Autumn light newborn
Swayed through the trees and lingered on the hill.
If things so lovely are, why labour still
To dream of something more than this I see ?
Do I remember tales of Galilee,
I who have slain my faith and freed my will ?
Let me forget dead faith, dead mystery,
Dead thoughts of things I cannot comprehend.
Enough the light mysterious in the tree,
Enough the friendship of my chosen friend.

Prayer

Let me not know how sins and sorrows glide
Along the sombre city of our rage,
Or why the sons of men are heavy-eyed.

Let me not know, except from printed page,
The pain of bitter love, of baffled pride,
Or sickness shadowing with a long presage.

Let me not know, since happy some have died
Quickly in youth or quietly in age,
How faint, how loud the bravest hearts have cried.

The Piper

A lad went piping through the Earth,
  Gladly, madly, merrily,
With a tune for death and a tune for birth,
  ` And a tune for lover's revelry.

He kissed the girls that sat alone
  With none to whisper, none to woo ;
Fired at his touch their faces shone,
  And beauty drenched them as the dew.

Old men who heard him danced again,
  And shuffled round with catching breath,
And those that lay on beds of pain
  Went dancing through the gates of death.

If only he could make us thrill
  Once more with mirth and melody !
I listened, but the street was still,
  And no one played for you and me.

1907

The Masque of the Magi

Three Kings have come to Bethlehem
With a trailing star in front of them.

MARY

What would you in this little place,
    You three bright kings ?

KINGS

Mother, we tracked the trailing star
Which brought us here from lands afar,
And we would look on his dear face
Round whom the Seraphs fold their wings.

MARY

But who are you, bright kings ?

CASPAR

Caspar am I : the rocky North
From storm and silence drave me forth
   Down to the blue and tideless sea.
I do not fear the tinkling sword,
For I am a great battle-lord,
   And love the horns of chivalry.
And I have brought thee splendid gold,
The strong man's joy, refined and cold.
   All hail, thou Prince of Galilee !

BALTHAZAR

I am Balthazar, Lord of Ind,
Where blows a soft and scented wind
   From Taprobane towards Cathay.
My children, who are tall and wise,
Stand by a tree with shutten eyes
   And seem to meditate or pray.
And these red drops of frankincense
Betoken man's intelligence.
   Hail, Lord of Wisdom, Prince of Day !

MELCHIOR

I am the dark man, Melchior,
And I shall live but little more
   Since I am old and feebly move.

My kingdom is a burnt-up land
Half buried by the drifting sand,
    So hot Apollo shines above.
What could I bring but simple myrrh
White blossom of the cordial fire ?
    Hail, Prince of Souls, and Lord of Love!

CHORUS OF ANGELS

O Prince of souls and Lord of Love,
O'er thee the purple-breasted dove
Shall watch with open silver wings,
    Thou King of Kings.
Suaviole o flos Virginum,
Apparuit Rex Gentium.

" Who art thou, little King of Kings ? "
His wondering mother sings.

.

To a Poet a Thousand Years Hence

I who am dead a thousand years,
    And wrote this sweet archaic song,
Send you my words for messengers
    The way I shall not pass along.

I care not if you bridge the seas,
    Or ride secure the cruel sky,
Or build consummate palaces
    Of metal or of masonry.

But have you wine and music still,
    And statues and a bright-eyed love,
And foolish thoughts of good and ill,
    And prayers to them who sit above ?

How shall we conquer ?   Like a wind
    That falls at eve our fancies blow,
And old Mæonides the blind
    Said it three thousand years ago.

O friend unseen, unborn, unknown,
  Student of our sweet English tongue,
Read out my words at night, alone :
  I was a poet, I was young.

Since I can never see your face,
  And never shake you by the hand,
I send my soul through time and space
  To greet you.   You will understand.

Heliodora

(*From Meleager*)

Why dost thou touch, O flower-fed bee,
　Heliodora's skin,
When open buds are asking thee
　To make thy home within ?

What parable art murmuring ?—
　That Eros makes man whole,
And turns the poison of his sting
　To sweetness in the soul ?

Is this your message, silly bee ?
　A dreamer takes it so.
Then home again !　Don't trouble me !
　I knew it long ago.

1908 ?

Love, the Baby

(From Meleager)

Let him be sold, I say ! Let him be sold,
Even while he slumbers at his mother's breast.
Why should I tend a thing so bad and bold,
A snub-nosed imp, a little scratching pest !
I find him always laughing through his tears :
He treats his mother badly ; won't be tamed,
Has baby wings behind him ; pries and peers,
Behaves unruly, chatters unashamed,—
A shocking monster ! Sailor men, this way !
Who wants a boy to carry off to sea ?
Oh dear, he's crying ! Come, I'll let you stay
Close to the heart of my Zenophile.

1908 ?

Ballad of the Londoner

Evening falls on the smoky walls,
  And the railings drip with rain,
And I will cross the old river
  To see my girl again.

The great and solemn-gliding tram,
  Love's still-mysterious car,
Has many a light of gold and white,
  And a single dark red star.

I know a garden in a street
  Which no one ever knew ;
I know a rose beyond the Thames,
  Where flowers are pale and few.

Resurrection

(By Piero degli Franceschi, at Borgo)

Sleep holds you, sons of war : you may not see
(You whose charmed heads sink heavy in your hands)
How 'twixt the budding and the barren tree
With glory in his staring eyes, he stands.
There's a sharp movement in this shivering morn
That blinds your senses while it breaks your power :
The Phœnix grips the eagle : Christ reborn
Bears high the standard.   Sleep a little hour :·
Sleep : it were best ye saw not those bright eyes
Prepared to wreck your world with errant flame,
And drive strong men to follow mysteries,
Voices, and winds, and things that have no name.
Dare you leave strength half-proved, duty half-done ?
Awake !   This God will hunt you from the sun !

Nov. 10, 1908

Dulce Lumen, Triste Numen, Suave Lumen Luminum

The town whose quiet veins are dark green sea,
The town whose flowers and forests are bright stone :
There it was the God came to you and me
In the signless depth of summer.   All alone
We lay, and half in dream
Gazed at the thin salt stream,
And heard the ripples talking lazily.

No verdurous growth, no sudden sharp decline
Of buds or leaves is there : the marble towers
Come rain, come cold, come snow or gay sunshine
Blossom eternally with graven flowers ;
Yet there the mild God came,
In silence, shod with flame,
Girdled with mystery and crowned with vine.

We lay in the sun and listened and we heard
Soft-treading feet and whispers in the air,
And thunder far away, like a god's word
Of dire import, and saw the noonday flare

And tall white palaces
Sway all with dizziness ;
The bells pealed faintly, and the water stirred

And Life stood still a moment, mists came swinging
Blindly before us ; suddenly we passed
The boundaries of joy : our hearts were ringing
True to the trembling world : we stood at last
Beyond the golden gate,
Masters of Time and Fate,
And knew the tune that Sun and Stars were singing.

For like two travellers on a hill, who stay
Viewing the smoke that dims the busy plains,
So, far away (sweet words are " far away " !)
We saw our life : and all its crooked lanes,
Dim cities and dark walls
Fell as a world that falls
And left us radiant in the Wind of Day.

An end, an end ! Again the leaden noon
Glowed, and hot Fever opened her red eyes,
And Misery came creeping out, and soon
We felt once more the sorrow of the Wise.
Come, friend ! We travel on
(That one brief vision gone)
Bravely, like men who see beyond the skies.

Nov. 20, 1908

Joseph and Mary

JOSEPH

Mary, art thou the little maid
    Who plucked me flowers in Spring ?
I know thee not : I feel afraid :
    Thou'rt strange this evening.

A sweet and rustic girl I won
    What time the woods were green ;
No woman with deep eyes that shone,
    And the pale brows of a Queen.

MARY (*inattentive to his words*)

A stranger came with feet of flame
    And told me this strange thing,—
For all I was a village maid
    My son should be a King.

JOSEPH

A King, dear wife.   Who ever knew
Of Kings in stables born !

MARY

Do you hear, in the dark and starlit blue
The clarion and the horn ?

JOSEPH

Mary, alas, lest grief and joy
    Have sent thy wits astray ;
But let me look on this my boy,
    And take the wraps away.

MARY

Behold the lad.

JOSEPH

        1 dare not gaze :
Light streams from every limb.

84

MARY

The winter sun has stored his rays,
And passed the fire to him.

Look Eastward, look! I hear a sound.
O Joseph, what do you see?

JOSEPH

The snow lies quiet on the ground
And glistens on the tree;

The sky is bright with a star's great light,
And clearly I behold
Three Kings descending yonder hill,
Whose crowns are crowns of gold.

O Mary, what do you hear and see
With your brow toward the West?

MARY

The snow lies glistening on the tree
And silent on Earth's breast;

And strong and tall, with lifted eyes
Seven shepherds walk this way,
And angels breaking from the skies
Dance, and sing hymns, and pray.

JOSEPH

I wonder much at these bright Kings;
The shepherds I despise.

MARY

You know not what a shepherd sings,
Nor see his shining eyes.

The Lover of Jalalu'ddin

My darling wandered through the house,
His bow upon the rebeck, light as flame.
Soft melodies he played, astray with sweet carouse,
Mad songs without a name.
Then, changing to a solemn mode and measure,
" Cupbearer, wine ! " he cried,
" Wine for the sons of pleasure,
The children of desire ! "
Forth from his corner came
The moonbright boy, and set the brimming bowl
Before us, with sweet reverence and grace.

My darling took the cup : over his face
Flowed truant flames. " Ye evil ghosts," he cried,
" I know my beauty : who is like to me ?
The sun of all the world, the Lover's pride,
I am, I was, shall be
With soul and spirit moving at my side."

Dec. 1908

Donde Estan ?

(*Fragment*)

I

We are they who dream no dreams,
Singers of arising day
Who undaunted,
Where the sword of reason gleams,
Follow hard, to hew away
The woods enchanted.
Through each dark and rustling byway
Evil things have fled before us :
We pursue them :
We have carved an open highway,
We have sung of Truth in chorus
As we slew them.

II

Though the shapes had something human,
Though sweet lips and eyes entreated
By their beauty :

Though processions of tall women
Looked and lured, we undefeated
Did our duty.
Though fair children, running after,
Held out hands of supplication,
Smiled and cried,
Yet we watched with bitter laughter
When delusion's fair creation
Smitten, died.

III

Where are they, the half-deceivers
Statue-forms and young men's fancies,
Gods of Greece ?
Dryads, where your groves and rivers,
Where thy chaste and woodland dances,
Artemis ?
Shadows, shadows ! None will follow
Cyprian maids ; or voices sighing
From the sea ;
Veiled is Iris, dark Apollo,
Dead the Queen who called the dying
Hecate.

*   *   •

V

Where are they who crushed the East
With ribaldry and song, and where
The lewd viziers ?
Where the girls who crowned the feast
For the Lords who had no care
Of blood or tears ?
Where the millions who, forgotten,
Fought for Selim's sultanate
And filled Gehenna ?
Where the sword ?—but dim and rotten
Lies the sword that cleft the gate
Of proud Vienna.

Feb. or Mar. 1909

The Town without a Market

There lies afar behind a western hill
The Town without a Market, white and still ;
For six feet long and not a third as high
Are those small habitations. There stood I,
Waiting to hear the citizens beneath
Murmur and sigh and speak through tongueless teeth.
When all the world lay burning in the sun
I heard their voices speak to me. Said one :
" Bright lights I loved and colours, I who find
That death is darkness, and has struck me blind."
Another cried : " I used to sing and play,
But here the world is silent, day by day."
And one : " On earth I could not see or hear,
But with my fingers touched what I was near,
And knew things round and soft, and brass from gold,
And dipped my hand in water, to feel cold,
And thought the grave would cure me, and was glad
When the time came to lose what joy I had."
Soon all the voices of a hundred dead
Shouted in wrath together. Some one said,
" I care not, but the girl was sweet to kiss
At evening in the meadows." " Hard it is,"

91

Another cried, " to hear no hunting horn.
Ah me ! the horse, the hounds, and the great grey morn
When I rode out a-hunting." And one sighed,
" I did not see my son before I died."
A boy said, " I was strong and swift to run :
Now they have tied my feet : what have I done ? "
A man, " But it was good to arm and fight
And storm their cities in the dead of night."
An old man said, " I read my books all day,
But death has taken all my books away."
And one, " The popes and prophets did not well
To cheat poor dead men with false hopes of hell.
Better the whips of fire that hiss and rend
Than painless void proceeding to no end."
I smiled to hear them restless, I who sough\
Peace. For I had not loved, I had not fought,
And books are vanities, and manly strength
A gathered flower. God grant us peace at length !
I heard no more, and turned to leave their town
Before the chill came, and the sun went down.
Then rose a whisper, and I seemed to know
A timorous man, buried long years ago.
" On Earth I used to shape the Thing that seems.
Master of all men, give me back my dreams.
Give me that world that never failed me then,
The hills I made and peopled with tall men,
The palace that I built and called my home,
My cities which could break the pride of Rome,
The three queens hidden in the sacred tree,
And those white clouds folk who sang to me.

92

O death, why hast thou covered me so deep ?
I was thy sister's child, the friend of Sleep."

Then said my heart, Death takes and cannot give.
Dark with no dream is hateful · let me live !

A Western Voyage

My friend the Sun—like all my friends
    Inconstant, lovely, far away—
Is out, and bright, and condescends
    To glory in our holiday.

A furious march with him I'll go
    And race him in the Western train,
And wake the hills I used to know
    And swim the Devon sea again.

I have done foolishly to tread
    The footway of the false moonbeams,
To light my lamp and call the dead
    And read their long black printed dreams.

I have done foolishly to dwell
    With Fear upon her desert isle,
To take my shadowgraph to Hell,
    And then to hope the shades would smue.

And since the light must fail me soon
  (But faster, faster, Western train !)
Proud meadows of the afternoon,
  I have remembered you again.

And I'll go seek through moor and dale
  A flower that wastrel winds caress ;
The bud is red and the leaves pale,
  The name of it Forgetfulness.

Then like the old and happy hills
  With frozen veins and fires outrun,
I'll wait the day when darkness kills
  My brother and good friend, the Sun.

Invitation

TO A YOUNG BUT LEARNED FRIEND TO ABANDON
ARCHÆOLOGY FOR THE MOMENT, AND PLAY ONCE
MORE WITH HIS NEGLECTED MUSE

In those good days when we were young and wise,
You spake to music, you with the thoughtful eyes,
And God looked down from heaven, pleased to hear
A young man's song arise so firm and clear.
Has Fancy died ?   The Morning Star gone cold ?
Why are you silent ?   Have we grown so old ?
Who sings upon Parnassus ?   He is dead,
The God to whom be prayers, not praises, said,
The sea-born, the Ionian.   There is one—
But he dreams deeper than the oaks of Clun.
(May summer keep his maids and meadows glad :
They hear no more the pipe of the Shropshire Lad !)
And our Tyrtæus ?   Strange that such a name
Already fades upon the mist of fame
With the smoke of Eastern armies.   But the third
Still knows the dreadful meaning of a word.
His gown is black and crimson : mystery
Veils all his speech, so wonderful is he.

These three remain, and voiceless you, and I.
—Come, the sweet radiance of our Spring is nigh.
Must I alone keep playing ?   Will not you,
Lord of the Measures, string your lyre anew ?
Lover of Greece, is this the richest store
You bring us,—withered leaves and dusty lore,
And broken vases widowed of their wine,
To brand you pedant while you stand divine ?
Decorous words beseem the learned lip,
But Poets have the nicer scholarship.
In English glades they watch the Cyprian glow
And all the Mænad melodies they know.
They hear strange voices in a London street,
And track the silver gleam of rushing feet ;
And these are things that come not to the view
Of slippered dons who read a codex through.
    O honeyed Poet, will you praise no more
The moonlit garden and the midnight shore ?
Brother, have you forgotten how to sing
The story of that weak and cautious king
Who reigned two hundred years in Trebizond ?
You who would ever strive to pierce beyond
Love's ecstasy, Life's vision, is it well
We should not know the tales you have to tell ?

War Song of the Saracens

We are they who come faster than fate : we are they who
    ride early or late :
We storm at your ivory gate : Pale Kings of the Sunset,
    beware !
Not on silk nor in samet we lie, not in curtained solemnity
    die
Among women who chatter and cry, and children who
    mumble a prayer.
But we sleep by the ropes of the camp, and we rise with a
    shout, and we tramp
With the sun or the moon for a lamp, and the spray of the
    wind in our hair.

From the lands, where the elephants are, to the forts of
    Merou and Balghar,
Our steel we have brought and our star to shine on the
    ruins of Rum.
We have marched from the Indus to Spain, and by God
    we will go there again ;
We have stood on the shore of the plain where the Waters
    of Destiny boom.

A mart of destruction we made at Jalula where men were
 afraid,
For death was a difficult trade, and the sword was a broker
 of doom ;

And the Spear was a Desert Physician who cured not a few
 of ambition,
And drave not a few to perdition with medicine bitter and
 strong :
And the shield was a grief to the fool and as bright as a
 desolate pool,
And as straight as the rock of Stamboul when their
 cavalry thundered along :
For the coward was drowned with the brave when our
 battle sheered up like a wave,
And the dead to the desert we gave, and the glory to God
 in our song.

The Ballad of Camden Town

I walked with Maisie long years back
  The streets of Camden Town,
I splendid in my suit of black,
  And she divine in brown.

Hers was a proud and noble face,
  A secret heart, and eyes
Like water in a lonely place
  Beneath unclouded skies.

A bed, a chest, a faded mat,
  And broken chairs a few,
Were all we had to grace our flat
  In Hazel Avenue.

But I could walk to Hampstead Heath,
  And crown her head with daisies,
And watch the streaming world beneath,
  And men with other Maisies.

When I was ill and she was pale
And empty stood our store,
She left the latchkey on its nail,
And saw me nevermore.

Perhaps she cast herself away
Lest both of us should drown:
Perhaps she feared to die, as they
Who die in Camden Town.

What came of her? The bitter nights
Destroy the rose and lily,
And souls are lost among the lights
Of painted Piccadilly.

What came of her? The river flows
So deep and wide and stilly,
And waits to catch the fallen rose
And clasp the broken lily.

I dream she dwells in London still
And breathes the evening air,
And often walk to Primrose Hill,
And hope to meet her there.

Once more together we will live,
For I will find her yet:
I have so little to forgive;
So much, I can't forget.

Gravis Dulcis Immutabilis

Come, let me kiss your wistful face
Where Sorrow curves her bow of pain,
And live sweet days and bitter days
With you, or wanting you again.

I dread your perishable gold :
Come near me now ; the years are few.
Alas, when you and I are old
I shall not want to look at you :

And yet come in.   I shall not dare
To gaze upon your countenance,
But I shall huddle in my chair,
Turn to the fire my fireless glance,

And listen, while that slow and grave
Immutable sweet voice of yours
Rises and falls, as falls a wave
In summer on forsaken shores.

Fountains

Soft is the collied night, and cool
The wind about the garden pool.
Here will I dip my burning hand
And move an inch of drowsy sand,
And pray the dark reflected skies
To fasten with their seal mine eyes.
A million million leagues away
Among the stars the goldfish play,
And high above the shadowed stars
Wave and float the nenuphars.

Dirge

If there be any grief
For those lost eremites
Who live where no man roams,
It is on Autumn nights
At falling of the leaf,
It is when pale October,
Relentless tree-disrober,
Conceals the smokeless homes.

Autumn is not so chill
Nor leaves so light in air,
Nor any wind as dim
Blowing from any where,
Nor fallen snow as still
As the boy who loved to wander
Singing till the forest yonder
Shouted in response to him.

My love has come to this—
And what of this to me ?
His eyes are eaten now,
My eyes he cannot see ;

Those gentle hands of his
Are taken by a stronger,
There is a hand no longer
To lay upon my brow.

Autumn has killed the rose ;
O mock him not with flowers
For they are troublesome :
Take him to pass the hours
Where the grey nettle grows.
Scantly his couch adorning
Let him who praised the morning
Lie here, till morning come.

*1909. Based on a poem
published in 1907 as " The
Young Poet "*

The Parrot

The old professor of Zoology
Shook his long beard and spake these words to me :
" Compare the Parrot with the Dove.   They are
In shape the same : in hue dissimilar.
The Indian bird, which may be sometimes seen
In red or black, is generally green.
His beak is very hard : it has been known
To crack thick nuts and penetrate a stone.
Alas that when you teach him how to speak
You find his head is harder than his beak.
The passionless Malay can safely drub
The pates of parrots with an iron club :
The ingenious fowls, like boys they beat at school,
Soon learn to recognize a Despot's rule.
　　Now if you'd train a parrot, catch him young
While soft the mouth and tractable the tongue.
Old birds are fools : they dodder in their speech,
More eager to forget than you to teach ;
They swear one curse, then gaze at you askance,
And all oblivion thickens in their glance.

　　Thrice blest whose parrot of his own accord
Invents new phrases to delight his Lord,

Who spurns the dull quotidian task and tries
Selected words that prove him good and wise.
Ah, once it was my privilege to know
A bird like this . . .
                    But that was long ago ! "

July 1909

Lord Arnaldos

¿ Quien hubiese tal ventura ?

The strangest of adventures,
That happen by the sea,
Befell to Lord Arnaldos
On the Evening of St. John ;
For he was out a-hunting—
A huntsman bold was he !—
When he beheld a little ship
And close to land was she.
Her cords were all of silver,
Her sails of cramasy ;
And he who sailed the little ship
Was singing at the helm :
The waves stood still to hear him,
The wind was soft and low ;
The fish who dwell in darkness
Ascended through the sea,
And all the birds in heaven
Flew down to his mast-tree.
Then spake the Lord Arnaldos,
(Well shall you hear his words !)

" Tell me for God's sake, sailor,
What song may that song be ? "
The sailor spake in answer,
And answer thus made he :
" I only tell my song to those
Who sail away with me."

A Miracle of Bethlehem

Scene : *A street of that village*

Three men with ropes, accosted by a stranger

THE STRANGER

I pray you, tell me where you go
With heads averted from the skies,
And long ropes trailing in the snow,
And resolution in your eyes.

THE FIRST MAN

I am a lover sick of love,
For scorn rewards my constancy ;
And now I hate the stars above,
Because my dear will naught of me.

THE SECOND MAN

I am a beggar man, and play
Songs with a splendid swing in them,
But I have seen no food to-day.
They want no song in Bethlehem.

THE THIRD MAN

I am an old man, Sir, and blind,
A child of darkness since my birth.
I cannot even call to mind
The beauty of the scheme of earth.

Therefore I sought to understand
A secret hid from mortal eyes,
So in a far and fragrant land
I talked with men accounted wise,

And I implored the Indian priest
For wisdom from his holy snake,
Yet am no wiser in the least,
And have not seen the darkness break.

STRANGER

And whither go ye now, unhappy three ?

111

The Three Men with Ropes

Sir, in our strange and special misery
We met this night, and swore in bitter pride
To sing one song together, friend with friend,
And then, proceeding to the country side,
To bind this cordage to a barren tree,
And face to face to give our lives an end,
And only thus shall we be satisfied.

(They make to continue their road)

The Stranger

Stay for a moment.   Great is your despair,
But God is kind.   What voice from over there ?

A Woman *(from a lattice)*

My lover, O my lover, come to me !

First Man

God with you.   *(He runs to the window)*

STRANGER

Ah, how swiftly gone is he!

MANY VOICES (*heard singing in a cottage*)

There is a softness in the night
A wonder in that splendid star
That fills us with delight,
Poor foolish working people that we are,
And only fit to keep
A little garden or a dozen sheep.

Old broken women at the fire
Have many ancient tales they sing,
How the whole world's desire
Should blossom here, and how a child should bring
New glory to his race
Though born in so contemptible a place.

Let all come in, if any brother go
In shame or hunger, cold or fear,
Through all this waste of snow.
To-night the Star, the Rose, the Song are near,
And still inside the door
Is full provision for another score.

(*The Beggar runs to them*)

H

THE STRANGER (*to the Blind Man*)

Do you not mean to share these joys ?

THE BLIND MAN

Aweary of this earthly noise
I pace my silent way.
Come you and help me tie this rope :
I would not lose my only hope.
Already clear the birds I hear,
Already breaks the day.

STRANGER

O foolish and most blind old man,
Where are those other two ?

THE BLIND MAN

Why, one is wed and t'other fed ;
Small thanks they gave to you.

STRANGER

To me no thanks are due.
Yet since I have some little power

Bequeathed me at this holy hour,
I tell you, friend, that God shall grant
This night to you your dearest want

THE BLIND MAN

Why this sweet odour ?   Why this flame ?
I am afraid.   What is your name ?

THE STRANGER

Ask your desire, for this great night
Is passing.

THE BLIND MAN

Sir, I ask my sight.

THE STRANGER

To see this earth ?   Or would you see
That hidden world which sent you me ?

115

The Blind Man

O sweet it were but once before I die
To track the bird about the windy sky,
Or watch the soft and changing grace
Imprinted on a human face.
Yet grant me that which most I struggled for,
Since I am old, and snow is on the ground.
On earth there's little to be found,
And I would bear with earth no more.
O gentle youth,
A fool am I, but let me see the Truth!

The Stranger

Gaze in my eyes.

The Blind Man

How can I gaze?
What song is that, and what these rays
Of splendour and this rush of wings?

The Stranger

These are the new celestial things.

116

THE BLIND MAN

Round the body of a child
A great dark flame runs wild.
What may this be ?

THE STRANGER

Look further, you shall see.

THE BLIND MAN

Out on the sea of time and far away
The Empires sail like ships, and many years
Scatter before them in a mist of spray :
And mountains rise like spears
Silver and sharp against the scarlet day.

THE STRANGER

It is most sure that God has heard his prayer.

(*The Stranger vanishes*)

117

The Beggar

*(Leading a troop of revellers from the house where
they were singing)*

Come, brothers, seek my friend and bring him in.
On such a night as this it were a sin
To leave the blind alone.

The Revellers

Greatly we fear lest he, still resolute,
Have wandered to the fields for poisoned fruit.

The Beggar

See here upon this stone . . .
He is all frozen . . . take him to a bed
And warm his hands.

The Revellers

O sorrow, he is dead !

Felo-de-se

The song of a man who was dead
Ere any had heard of his song,
Or had seen this his ultimate song,
With the lines of it written in red,
And the sound of it steady and strong.
When you hear it, you know I am dead.

Not because I was weary of life
As pallid poets are :
My star was a conquering star,
My element strife.
I am young, I am strong, I am brave,
It is therefore I go to the grave.

Now to life and to life's desire,
And to youth and the glory of youth,
Farewell, for I go to acquire,
By the one road left me, Truth.
Though a great God slay me with fire
I will shout till he answer me.   Why ?

(One soul and a Universe, why ?)
And for this it is pleasant to die.

For years and years I have slumbered,
And slumber was heavy and sweet,
But the last few moments are numbered,
Like trampling feet that beat.
I shall walk with the stars in their courses,
And hear very soon, very soon,
The voice of the forge of the Forces,
And ride on the ridge of the moon,
And sing a celestial tune.

The Welsh Sea

Far out across Carnarvon bay,
  Beneath the evening waves,
The ancient dead begin their day
  And stream among the graves.

Listen, for they of ghostly speech,
  Who died when Christ was born,
May dance upon the yellow beach
  That once was yellow corn.

And you may learn of Dyfed's reign,
  And dream Nemedian tales
Of Kings who sailed in ships from Spain
  And lent their swords to Wales.

Listen, for like a slow, green snake
  The Ocean twists and stirs,
And whispers how the dead men wake
  And call across the years.

In Memoriam

I never shall forget that night—
    Mid-April, four years gone :
Nor how your eyes were bright, too bright,
    And how the pavement shone.

Death on you now, death on your brow,
    Death on your eyes so fair,
Death with his thin shadow hands
    Combing out your hair.

O eyes long shut and lip to lip
    Fastened no more to sing :
Old winter turned you in his grip
    And icy blew your spring.

Old winter had you by the throat
    You could not speak to me
Save in a low and whispered note
    As through a shell the sea.

Death on you now, death on your brow,
    Death on your eyes so fair,
Death with his thin shadow hands
    Combing out your hair.

1910

Opportunity

(*From Machiavelli*)

" But who art thou, with curious beauty graced,
O woman, stamped with some bright heavenly seal ?
Why go thy feet on wings, and in such haste ? "

" I am that maid whose secret few may steal
Called Opportunity.   I hasten by
Because my feet are treading on a wheel,

" Being more swift to run than birds to fly.
And rightly on my feet my wings I wear,
To blind the sight of those who track and spy ;

" Rightly in front I hold my scattered hair
To veil my face, and down my breast to fall,
Lest men should know my name when I am there ;

" And leave behind my back no wisp at all
Fo. eager folk to clutch, what time I glide
So near, and turn, and pass beyond recall."

" Tell me ; who is that Figure at thy side ? "
" Penitence. Mark this well that by degree
Who lets me go must keep her for his bride.

" And thou hast spent much time in talk with me
Busied with thoughts and fancies vainly grand,
Nor hast remarked, O fool, neither dost see
How lightly I have fled beneath thy hand."

No Coward's Song

I am afraid to think about my death,
When it shall be, and whether in great pain
I shall rise up and fight the air for breath
Or calmly wait the bursting of my brain.

I am no coward who could seek in fear
A folk-lore solace or sweet Indian tales :
I know dead men are deaf and cannot hear
The singing of a thousand nightingales.

I know dead men are blind and cannot see
The friend that shuts in horror their big eyes,
And they are witless—O, I'd rather be
A living mouse than dead as a man dies.

Pillage

They will trample our gardens to mire, they will bury our
    city in fire ;
Our women await their desire, our children the clang of
    the chain.
Our grave-eyed judges and lords they will bind by the
    neck with cords,
And harry with whips and swords till they perish of shame
    or pain,
And the great lapis lazuli dome where the gods of our
    race had a home
Will break like a wave from the foam, and shred into
    fiery rain.

No more on the long summer days shall we walk in the
    meadow-sweet ways
With the teachers of music and phrase, and the masters
    of dance and design.
No more when the trumpeter calls shall we feast in the
    white-light halls ;
For stayed are the soft footfalls of the moon-browed
    bearers of wine,

And lost are the statues of Kings and of Gods with great
glorious wings,
And an empire of beautiful things, and the lips of the love
who was mine.

We have vanished, but not into night, though our manhood
we sold to delight,
Neglecting the chances of fight, unfit for the spear and
the bow.
We are dead, but our living was great : we are dumb, but
a song of our State
Will roam in the desert and wait, with its burden of long,
long ago,
Till a scholar from sea-bright lands unearth from the years
and the sands
Some image with beautiful hands, and know what we want
him to know.

The Ballad of Zacho

(A Greek Legend)

Zacho the King rode out of old
  (And truth is what I tell)
With saddle and spurs and a rein of gold
  To find the door of Hell.

And round around him surged the dead
  With soft and lustrous eyes.
" Why came you here, old friend ? " they said :
  " Unwise . . . unwise . . . unwise !

" You should have left to the prince your son
  Spurs and saddle and rein :
Your bright and morning days are done ;
  You ride not out again."

" I came to greet my friends who fell
  Sword-scattered from my side ;
And when I've drunk the wine of Hell
  I'll out again and ride ! "

But Charon rose and caught his hair
   In fingers sharp and long.
" Loose me, old ferryman : play fair :
   Try if my arm be strong."

Thrice drave he hard on Charon's breast,
   And struck him thrice to ground,
Till stranger ghosts came out o' the west
   And sat like stars around.

And thrice old Charon rose up high
   And seized him as before.
" Loose me ! a broken man am I,
   And fight with you no more."

" Zacho, arise, my home is near ;
   I pray you walk with me :
I've hung my tent so full of fear
   You well may shake to see.

" Home to my home come they who fight,
   Who fight but not tc win :
Without, my tent is black as night,
   And red as fire within.

" Though winds blow cold and I grow old,
   My tent is fast and fair :
The pegs are dead men's stout right arms,
   The cords, their golden hair."

I

Pavlovna in London

I listened to the hunger-hearted clown,
  Sadder than he : I heard a woman sing,—
A tall dark woman in a scarlet gown—
  And saw those golden toys the jugglers fling.
I found a tawdry room and there sat I,
    There angled for each murmur soft and strange,
    The pavement-cries from darkness and below :
I watched the drinkers laugh, the lovers sigh,
    And thought how little all the world would change
    If clowns were audience, and we the Show.

What starry music are they playing now ?
  What dancing in this dreary theatre ?
Who is she with the moon upon her brow,
  And who the fire-foot god that follows her ?—
Follows among those unbelieved-in trees
    Back-shadowing in their parody of light
    Across the little cardboard balustrade ;
And we, like that poor Faun who pipes and flees,
    Adore their beauty, hate it for too bright,
    And tremble, half in rapture, half afraid.

Play on, O furtive and heartbroken Faun !
What is your thin dull pipe for such as they ?
I know you blinded by the least white dawn,
    And dare you face their quick and quivering Day ?
Dare you, like us, weak but undaunted men,
    Reliant on some deathless spark in you
        Turn your dull eyes to what the gods desire,
Touch the light finger of your goddess ; then
    After a second's flash of gold and blue,
    Drunken with that divinity, expire ?

O dance, Diana, dance, Endymion,
    Till calm ancestral shadows lay their hands
Gently across mine eyes : in days long gone
    Have I not danced with gods in garden lands ?
I too a wild unsighted atom borne
    Deep in the heart of some heroic boy
        Span in the dance ten thousand years ago,
And while his young eyes glittered in the morn
    Something of me felt something of his joy,
    And longed to rule a body, and to know.

Singer long dead and sweeter-lipped than I,
    In whose proud line the soul-dark phrases burn,
Would you could praise their passionate symmetry,
    Who loved the colder shapes, the Attic urn.

But your far song, my faint one, what are they,
  And what their dance and faery thoughts and ours
    Or night abloom with splendid stars and pale ?
'Tis an old story that sweet flowers decay,
  And dreams, the noblest, die as soon as flowers,
  And dancers, all the world of them, must fail.

The Sentimentalist

There lies a photograph of you
   Deep in a box of broken things.
This was the face I loved and knew
   Five years ago, when life had wings;

Five years ago, when through a town
   Of bright and soft and shadowy bowers
We walked and talked and trailed our gown
   Regardless of the cinctured hours.

The precepts that we held I kept;
   Proudly my ways with you I went:
We lived our dreams while others slept,
   And did not shrink from sentiment.

Now I go East and you stay West
   And when between us Europe lies
I shall forget what I loved best,
   Away from lips and hands and eyes.

But we were Gods then : we were they
Who laughed at fools, believed in friends,
And drank to all that golden day
Before us, which this poem ends.

Don Juan in Hell

(From Baudelaire)

The night Don Juan came to pay his fees
    To Charon, by the caverned water's shore,
A beggar, proud-eyed as Antisthenes,
    Stretched out his knotted fingers on the oar.

Mournful, with drooping breasts and robes unsewn
    The shapes of women swayed in ebon skies,
Trailing behind him with a restless moan
    Like cattle herded for a sacrifice.

Here, grinning for his wage, stood Sganarelle,
    And here Don Luis pointed, bent and dim,
To show the dead who lined the holes of Hell,
    This was that impious son who mocked at him.

The hollow-eyed, the chaste Elvira came,
    Trembling and veiled, to view her traitor spouse.
Was it one last bright smile she thought to claim,
    Such as made sweet the morning of his vows ?

A great stone man rose like a tower on board,
  Stood at the helm and cleft the flood profound :
But the calm hero, leaning on his sword,
  Gazed back, and would not offer one look round.

The Ballad of Iskander

Aflatun and Aristu and King Iskander
Are Plato, Aristotle, Alexander

Sultan Iskander sat him down
On his golden throne, in his golden crown,
And shouted, " Wine and flute-girls three,
And the Captain, ho ! of my ships at sea."

He drank his bowl of wine ; he kept
The flute-girls dancing till they wept,
Praised and kissed their painted lips,
And turned to the Captain of All his Ships

And cried, " O Lord of my Ships that go
From the Persian Gulf to the Pits of Snow,
Inquire for men unknown to man ! "
Said Sultan Iskander of Yoonistan.

" Daroosh is dead, and I am King
Of Everywhere and Everything :
Yet leagues and leagues away for sure
The lion-hearted dream of war.

" Admiral, I command you sail !
Take you a ship of silver mail,
And fifty sailors, young and bold,
And stack provision deep in the hold,

" And seek out twenty men that know
All babel tongues which flaunt and flow ;
And stay !   Impress those learned two,
Old Aflatun, and Aristu.

" And set your prow South-western ways
A thousand bright and dimpling days,
And find me lion-hearted Lords
With breasts to feed Our rusting swords."

The Captain of the Ships bowed low.
" Sir," he replied, " I will do so."
And down he rode to the harbour mouth,
To choose a boat to carry him South.

And he launched a ship of silver mail,
With fifty lads to hoist the sail,
And twenty wise—all tongues they knew,
And Aflatun, and Aristu.

There had not dawned the second day
But the glittering galleon sailed away,
And through the night like one great bell
The marshalled armies sang farewell.

138

In twenty days the silver ship
Had passed the Isle of Serendip,
And made the flat Araunian coasts
Inhabited, at noon, by Ghosts.

In thirty days the ship was far
Beyond the land of Calcobar,
Where men drink Dead Men's Blood for wine,
And dye their beards alizarine.

But on the hundredth day there came
Storm with his windy wings aflame,
And drave them out to that Lone Sea
Whose shores are near Eternity.

    *   *   *

For seven years and seven years
Sailed those forgotten mariners,
Nor could they spy on either hand
The faintest level of good red land.

Bird or fish they saw not one ;
There swam no ship beside their own,
And day-night long the lilied Deep
Lay round them, with its flowers asleep.

The beams began to warp and crack,
The silver plates turned filthy black,
And drooping down on the carven rails
Hung those once lovely silken sails.

And all the great ship's crew who were
Such noble lads to do and dare
Grew old and tired of the changeless sky
And laid them down on the deck to die.

And they who spake all tongues there be
Made antics with solemnity,
Or closely huddled each to each
Talked ribald in a foreign speech

And Aflatun and Aristu
Let their Beards grow, and their Beards grew
Round and about the mainmast tree
Where they stood still, and watched the sea.

And day by day their Captain grey
Knelt on the rotting poop to pray :
And yet despite ten thousand prayers
They saw no ship that was not theirs.

* * *

When thrice the seven years had passed
They saw a ship, a ship at last !
Untarnished glowed its silver mail,
Windless bellied its silken sail.

With a shout the grizzled sailors rose
Cursing the years of sick repose,
And they who spake in tongues unknown
Gladly reverted to their own.

The Captain leapt and left his prayers
And hastened down the dust-dark stairs,
And taking to hand a brazen Whip
He woke to life the long dead ship.

But Aflatun and Aristu,
Who had no work that they could do,
Gazed at the stranger Ship and Sea
With their beards around the mainmast tree.

Nearer and nearer the new boat came,
Till the hands cried out on the old ship's shame—
" Silken sail to a silver boat,
We too shone when we first set float ! "

Swifter and swifter the bright boat sped,
But the hands spake thin like men long dead—
" *How striking like that boat were we*
In the days, sweet days, when we put to sea."

The ship all black and the ship all white
Met like the meeting of day and night,
Met, and there lay serene dark green
A twilight yard of the sea between.

And the twenty masters of foreign speech
Of every tongue they knew tried each ;
Smiling, the silver Captain heard,
But shook his head and said nc word.

141

Then Aflatun and Aristu
Addressed the silver Lord anew,
Speaking their language of Yoonistan
Like countrymen to a countryman.

And " Whence," they cried, " O Sons of Pride,
Sail you the dark eternal tide ?
Lie your halls to the South or North,
And who is the King that sent you forth ? "

" We live," replied that Lord with a smile,
" A mile beyond the millionth mile.
We know not South and we know not North,
And *SULTAN ISKANDER* sent us forth."

Said Aristu to Aflatun—
" Surely our King, despondent soon,
Has sent this second ship to find
Unconquered tracts of humankind."

But Aflatun turned round on him
Laughing a bitter laugh and grim.
" Alas," he said, " O Aristu,
A white weak thin old fool are you.

" And does yon silver Ship appear
As she had journeyed twenty year ?
And has that silver Captain's face
A mortal or Immortal grace ?

" Theirs is the land (as well I know)
Where live the Shapes of Things Below :
Theirs is the country where they keep
The Images men see in Sleep.

" Theirs is the Land beyond the Door,
And theirs the old ideal shore.
They steer our ship : behold our crew
Ideal, and our Captain too.

" And lo ! beside that mainmast tree
Two tall and shining forms I see,
And they are what we ought to be,
Yet we are they, and they are we."

He spake, and some young Zephyr stirred
The two ships touched : no sound was heard ;
The Black Ship crumbled into air ;
Only the Phantom Ship was there.

And a great cry rang round the sky
Of glorious singers sweeping by,
And calm and fair on waves that shone
The Silver Ship sailed on and on.

The Golden Journey to Samarkand

PROLOGUE

We who with songs beguile your pilgrimage
 And swear that Beauty lives though lilies die,
We Poets of the proud old lineage
 Who sing to find your hearts, we know not why,—

What shall we tell you ? Tales, marvellous tales
 Of ships and stars and isles where good men rest,
Where nevermore the rose of sunset pales,
 And winds and shadows fall toward the West :

And there the world's first huge white-bearded kings
 In dim glades sleeping, murmur in their sleep,
And closer round their breasts the ivy clings,
 Cutting its pathway slow and red and deep.

II

And how beguile you ? Death has no repose
 Warmer and deeper than that Orient sand
Which hides the beauty and bright faith of those
 Who made the Golden Journey to Samarkand.

And now they wait and whiten peaceably,
  Those conquerors, those poets, those so fair :
They know time comes, not only you and I,
  But the whole world shall whiten, here or there ;

When those long caravans that cross the plain
  With dauntless feet and sound of silver bells
Put forth no more for glory or for gain,
  Take no more solace from the palm-girt wells.

When the great markets by the sea shut fast
  All that calm Sunday that goes on and on :
When even lovers find their peace at last,
  And Earth is but a star, that once had shone.

Epilogue

At the Gate of the Sun, Bagdad, in olden time

THE MERCHANTS (*together*)

Away, for we are ready to a man !
  Our camels sniff the evening and are glad.
Lead on, O Master of the Caravan :
  Lead on the Merchant-Princes of Bagdad.

THE CHIEF DRAPER

Have we not Indian carpets dark as wine,
  Turbans and sashes, gowns and bows and veils,
And broideries of intricate design,
  And printed hangings in enormous bales ?

THE CHIEF GROCER

We have rose-candy, we have spikenard,
  Mastic and terebinth and oil and spice,
And such sweet jams meticulously jarred
  As God's own Prophet eats in Paradise.

146

THE PRINCIPAL JEWS

And we have manuscripts in peacock styles
By Ali of Damascus ; we have swords
Engraved with storks and apes and crocodiles,
And heavy beaten necklaces, for Lords.

THE MASTER OF THE CARAVAN

But you are nothing but a lot of Jews.

THE PRINCIPAL JEWS

Sir, even dogs have daylight, and we pay.

THE MASTER OF THE CARAVAN

But who are ye in rags and rotten shoes,
You dirty-bearded, blocking up the way ?

THE PILGRIMS

We are the Pilgrims, master ; we shall go
Always a little further : it may be
Beyond that last blue mountain barred with snow,
Across that angry or that glimmering sea,

White on a throne or guarded in a cave
There lives a prophet who can understand
Why men were born : but surely we are brave,
Who make the Golden Journey to Samarkand.

THE CHIEF MERCHANT

We gnaw the nail of hurry.   Master, away !

ONE OF THE WOMEN

O turn your eyes to where your children stand.
Is not Bagdad the beautiful ?   O stay !

THE MERCHANTS (*in chorus*)

We take the Golden Road to Samarkand.

AN OLD MAN

Have you not girls and garlands in your homes,
Eunuchs and Syrian boys at your command ?
Seek not excess : God hateth him who roams !

148

THE MERCHANTS (*in chorus*)

We make the Golden Journey to Samarkand.

A PILGRIM WITH A BEAUTIFUL VOICE

Sweet to ride forth at evening from the wells
When shadows pass gigantic on the sand,
And softly through the silence beat the bells
Along the Golden Road to Samarkand.

A MERCHANT

We travel not for trafficking alone :
    By hotter winds our fiery hearts are fanned :
For lust of knowing what should not be known
We make the Golden Journey to Samarkand.

THE MASTER OF THE CARAVAN

Open the gate, O watchman of the night !

THE WATCHMAN

    Ho, travellers, I open.   For what land
Leave you the dim-moon city of delight ?

149

THE MERCHANTS (*with a shout*)

We make the Golden Journey to Samarkand.

[*The Caravan passes through the gate*]

THE WATCHMAN (*consoling the women*)

What would ye, ladies ?   It was ever thus.
Men are unwise and curiously planned.

A WOMAN

They have their dreams, and do not think of us.

VOICES OF THE CARAVAN (*in the distance, singing*)

We make the Golden Journey to Samarkand.

Gates of Damascus

Four great gates has the city of Damascus,
   And four Grand Wardens, on their spears reclining,
All day long stand like tall stone men
   And sleep on the towers when the moon is shining.

This is the song of the East Gate Warden
When he locks the great gate and smokes in his garden.

Postern of Fate, the Desert Gate, Disaster's Cavern, Fort
   of Fear,
The Portal of Bagdad am I, the Doorway of Diarbekir.

The Persian Dawn with new desires may net the flushing
   mountain spires :
But my gaunt buttress still rejects the suppliance of those
   mellow fires.

Pass not beneath, O Caravan, or pass not singing.   Have
   you heard
That silence where the birds are dead yet something pipeth
   like a bird ?

Pass not beneath! Men say there blows in stony deserts
still a rose
But with no scarlet to her leaf—and from whose heart no
perfume flows.

Wilt thou bloom red where she buds pale, thy sister rose?
Wilt thou not fail
When noonday flashes like a flail? Leave nightingale
the caravan!

Pass then, pass all! "Bagdad!" ye cry, and down the
billows of blue sky
Ye beat the bell that beats to hell, and who shall thrust ye
back? Not I.

The Sun who flashes through the head and paints the
shadows green and red,—
The Sun shall eat thy fleshless dead, O Caravan, O Caravan!

And one who licks his lips for thirst with f-vered eyes shall
face in fear
The palms that wave, the streams that burst, his last
mirage, O Caravan!

And one—the bird-voiced Singing-man—shall fall behind
thee, Caravan!
And God shall meet him in the night, and he shall sing as
best he can.

And one the Bedouin shall slay, and one, sand-stricken on
    the way
Go dark and blind; and one shall say—" How lonely is
    the Caravan ! "

Pass out beneath, O Caravan, Doom's Caravan, Death's
    Caravan !
I had not told ye, fools, so much, save that I heard your
    Singing-man.

    This was sung by the West Gate's keeper
    When heaven's hollow dome grew deeper.

I am the gate toward the sea : O sailor men, pass out from
    me !
I hear you high on Lebanon, singing the marvels of the sea.

The dragon-green, the luminous, the dark, the serpent-
    haunted sea,
The snow-besprinkled wine of earth, the white-and-blue-
    flower foaming sea.

Beyond the sea are towns with towers, carved with lions
    and lily flowers,
And not a soul in all those lonely streets to while away
    the hours.

Beyond the towns, an isle where, bound, a naked giant bites
the ground :
The shadow of a monstrous wing looms on his back : and
still no sound.

Beyond the isle a rock that screams like madmen shouting
in their dreams,
From whose dark issues night and day blood crashes in a
thousand streams.

Beyond the rock is Restful Bay, where no wind breathes or
ripple stirs,
And there on Roman ships, they say, stand rows of metal
mariners.

Beyond the bay in utmost West old Solomon the Jewish
King
Sits with his beard upon his breast, and grips and guards
his magic ring :

And when that ring is stolen, he will rise in outraged
majesty,
And take the World upon his back, and fling the World
beyond the sea.

This is the song of the North Gate's master,
Who singeth fast, but drinketh faster.

I am the gay Aleppo Gate : a dawn, a dawn and thou art
there :
Eat not thy heart with fear and care, O brother of the beast
we hate !

Thou hast not many miles to tread, nor other foes than fleas
to dread ;
Homs shall behold thy morning meal and Hama see thee
safe in bed.

Take to Aleppo filigrane, and take them paste of apricots,
And coffee tables botched with pearl, and little beaten
brassware pots :

And thou shalt sell thy wares for thrice the Damascene
retailers' price,
And buy a fat Armenian slave who smelleth odorous and nice.

Some men of noble stock were made : some glory in the
murder-blade :
Some praise a Science or an Art, but I like honourable
Trade !

Sell them the rotten, buy the ripe ! Their heads are weak ;
their pockets burn.
Aleppo men are mighty fools. Salaam Aleikum ! Safe
return !

This is the song of the South Gate Holder,
A silver man, but his song is older.

I am the Gate that fears no fall : the Mihrab of Damascus
wall,
The bridge of booming Sinai : the Arch of Allah all in all.

O spiritual pilgrim rise : the night has grown her single
horn :
The voices of the souls unborn are half adream with
Paradise.

To Meccah thou hast turned in prayer with aching heart
and eyes that burn :
Ah Hajji, whither wilt thou turn when thou art there,
when thou art there ?

God be thy guide from camp to camp : God be thy shade
from well to well ;
God grant beneath the desert stars thou hear the Prophet's
camel bell.

And God shall make thy body pure, and give thee knowledge
to endure
This ghost-life's piercing phantom-pain, and bring thee out
to Life again.

And God shall make thy soul a Glass where eighteen
thousand Æons pass,
And thou shalt see the gleaming Worlds as men see dew
upon the grass.

And son of Islam, it may be that thou shalt learn at journey's
end
Who walks thy garden eve on eve, and bows his head, and
calls thee Friend.

Yasmin

A GHAZEL

How splendid in the morning glows the lily : with what
   grace he throws
His supplication to the rose : do roses nod the head, Yasmin?

But when the silver dove descends I find the little flower of
   friends
Whose very name that sweetly ends I say when I have said,
   Yasmin.

The morning light is clear and cold : I dare not in that
   light behold
A whiter light, a deeper gold, a glory too far shed, Yasmin.

But when the deep red eye of day is level with the lone
   highway,
And some to Meccah turn to pray, and I toward thy bed,
   Yasmin ;

Or when the wind beneath the moon is drifting like a soul aswoon,
And harping planets talk love's tune with milky wings outspread, Yasmin,

Shower down thy love, O burning bright ! For one night or the other night
Will come the Gardener in white, and gathered flowers are dead, Yasmin.

Saadabad

I

Let us deal kindly with a heart of old by sorrow torn :
Come with Nedim to Saadabad, my love, this silver morn :
I hear the boatmen singing from our caïque on the Horn,
Waving cypress, waving cypress, let us go to Saadabad !

We shall watch the Sultan's fountains ripple, rumble,
    splash and rise
Over terraces of marble, under the blue balconies,
Leaping through the plaster dragon's hollow mouth and
    empty eyes :
Waving cypress, waving cypress, let us go to Saadabad.

Lie a little to your mother : tell her you must out to pray,
And we'll slink along the alleys, thieves of all a summer
    day,
Down to the worn old watersteps, and then, my love, away
O my cypress, waving cypress, let us go to Saadabad.

You and I, and with us only some poor lover in a dream :
I and you—perhaps one minstrel who will sing beside the
stream.
Ah Nedim will be the minstrel, and the lov 'r be Nedim,
Waving cypress, waving cypress, when we go to Saadabad !

II

Down the Horn Constantinople fades and flashes in the blue,
Rose of cities dropping with the heavy summer's burning
dew,
Fading now as falls the Orient evening round the sky and
you,
Fading into red and silver as we row to Saadabad.

Banish then, O Grecian eyes, the passion of the waiting
West !
Shall God's holy monks not enter on a day God knoweth
best
To crown the Roman king again, and hang a cross upon his
breast ?
Daughter of the Golden Islands, come away to Saadabad.

And a thousand swinging steeples shall begin as they began
When Heraclius rode home from the wrack of Ispahan,
Naked captives pulled behind him, double eagles in the van—
But is that a tale for lovers on the way to Saadabad ?

Rather now shall you remember how of old two such as we,
You like her the laughing mistress of a poet, him or me,
Came to find the flowery lawns that give the soul tranquil-
lity :
Let the boatmen row no longer—for we land at Saadabad.

See you not that moon-dim caïque with the lovers at the
prow,
Straining eyes and aching lips, and touching hands as we do
now,
See you not the turbaned shadows passing, whence ? and
moving, how ?
Are the ghosts of all the Moslems floating down to
Saadabad ?

*   *   *

Broken fountains, phantom waters, nevermore to glide and
gleam
From the dragon-mouth in plaster sung of old by old
Nedim,
Beautiful and broken fountains, keep you still your Sultan's
dream,
Or remember how his poet took a girl to Saadabad ?

The Hammam Name

(*From a poem by a Turkish lady*)

Winsome Torment rose from slumber, rubbed his eyes, and
    went his way
Down the street towards the Hammam. Goodness
    gracious ! people say,
What a handsome countenance ! The sun has risen twice
    to-day !
And as for the Undressing Room it quivered in dismay.
With the glory of his presence see the window panes perspire,
And the water in the basin boils and bubbles with desire.

Now his lovely cap is treated like a lover : off it goes !
Next his belt the boy unbuckles ; down it falls, and at his
    toes
All the growing heap of garments buds and blossoms like
    a rose.
Last of all his shirt came flying. Ah, I tremble to disclose
How the shell came off the almond, how the lily showed its
    face,
How I saw a silver mirror taken flashing from its case.

He was gazed upon so hotly that his body grew too hot,
So the bathman seized the adorers and expelled them on
the spot ;
Then the desperate shampooer his propriety forgot,
Stumbled when he brought the pattens, fumbled when he
tied a knot,
And remarked when musky towels had obscured his idol's
hips,
See Love's Plenilune, Mashallah, in a partial eclipse !

Desperate the loofah wriggled : soap was melted instantly :
All the bubble hearts were broken.   Yes, for them as well
as me,
Bitterness was born of beauty ; as for the shampooer, he
Fainted, till a jug of water set the Captive Reason free.
Happy bath ! The baths of heaven cannot wash their
spotted moon :
You are doing well with this one.   Not a spot upon him
soon !

Now he leaves the luckless bath for fear of setting it alight ;
Seizes on a yellow towel growing yellower in fright,
Polishes the pearly surface till it burns disastrous bright,
And a bathroom window shatters in amazement at the
sight.
Like the fancies of a dreamer frail and soft his garments
shine
As he robes a mirror body shapely as a poet's line.

Now upon his cup of coffee see the lips of Beauty bent :
And they perfume him with incense and they sprinkle him
    with scent,
Call him Bey and call him Pasha, and receive with deep
    content
The gratuities he gives them, smiling and indifferent.
Out he goes : the mirror strains to kiss her darling ; out
    he goes !
Since the flame is out, the water can but freeze.
                        The water froze.

In Phæacia

Had I that haze of streaming blue,
  That sea below, the summer faced,
I'd work and weave a dress for you
  And kneel to clasp it round your waist,
And broider with those burning bright
  Threads of the Sun across the sea,
And bind it with the silver light
  That wavers in the olive tree.

Had I the gold that like a river
  Pours through our garden, eve by eve,
Our garden that goes on for ever
  Out of the world, as we believe ;
Had I that glory on the vine
  That splendour soft on tower and town,
I'd forge a crown of that sunshine,
  And break before your feet the crown.

Through the great pinewood I have been
  An hour before the lustre dies,
Nor have such forest-colours seen
  As those that glimmer in your eyes.

Ah, misty woodland, down whose deep
 And twilight paths I love to stroll
To meadows quieter than sleep
 And pools more secret than the soul !

Could I but steal that awful throne
 Ablaze with dreams and songs and stars
Where sits Night, a man of stone,
 On the frozen mountain spars
I'd cast him down, for he is old,
 And set my Lady there to rule,
Gowned with silver, crowned with gold,
 And in her eyes the forest pool.

Epithalamion

Smile then, children, hand in hand
Bright and white as the summer snow,
Or that young King of the Grecian land,
Who smiled on Thetis, long ago,—
So long ago when, heart aflame,
The grave and gentle Peleus came
To the shore where the halcyon flies
To wed the maiden of his devotion,
The dancing lady with sky-blue eyes,
Thetis, the darling of Paradise,
The daughter of old Ocean.
Seas before her rise and break,
Dolphins tumble in her wake
Along the sapphire courses :
With Tritons ablow on their pearly shells
With a plash of waves and a clash of bells
From the glimmering house where her Father dwells
She drives his white-tail horses !
And the boys of heaven gowned and crowned,
Have Aphrodite to lead them round,
Aphrodite with hair unbound

Her silver breasts adorning.
Her long, her soft, her streaming hair,
Falls on a silver breast laid bare
By the stir and swing of the sealit air
And the movement of the morning.

Hyali

Στὸ Γυαλὶ, στὸ γαλάζιο βράχο

Island in blue of summer floating on,
  Little brave sister of the Sporades,
Hail and farewell ! I pass, and thou art gone,
  So fast in fire the great boat beats the seas.

But slowly fade, soft Island ! Ah to know
  Thy town and who the gossips of thy town,
What flowers flash in thy meadows, what winds blow
  Across thy mountain when the sun goes down.

There is thy market, where the fisher throws
  His gleaming fish that gasp in the death-bright dawn :
And there thy Prince's house, painted old rose,
  Beyond the olives, crowns its slope of lawn.

And is thy Prince so rich that he displays
  At festal board the flesh of sheep and kine ?
Or dare he—summer days are long hot days—
  Load up with Asian snow his Coan wine ?

Behind a rock, thy harbour, whence a noise
  Of tarry sponge-boats hammered lustily :
And from that little rock thy naked boys
  Like burning arrows shower upon the sea.

And there by the old Greek chapel—there beneath
  A thousand poppies that each sea-wind stirs
And cyclamen, as honied and white as death,
  Dwell deep in earth the elder islanders.

          •   •   •

Thy name I know not, Island, but *his* name
  I know, and why so proud thy mountain stands,
And what thy happy secret, and Who came
  Drawing his painted galley up thy sands.

For my Gods—Trident Gods who deep and pale
  Swim in the Latmian Sound, have murmured thus :
" To such an island came with a pompous sail
  On his first voyage young Herodotus."

Since then—tell me no tale how Romans built,
  Saracens plundered—or that bearded lords
Rowed by to fight for Venice, and here spilt
  Their blood across the bay that keeps their swords.

That old Greek day was all thy history :
  For that did Ocean poise thee as a flower.
Farewell : this boat attends not such as thee :
  Farewell : I was thy lover for an hour !

Farewell ! But I who call upon thy caves
  Am far like thee,—like thee, unknown and poor,
And yet my words are music as thy waves,
  And like thy rocks shall down through time endure.

Santorin

(*A Legend of the Ægean*)

" Who are you, Sea Lady,
And where in the seas are we ?
I have too long been steering
By the flashes in your eyes.
Why drops the moonlight through my heart,
And why so quietly
Go the great engines of my boat
As if their souls were free ? "
" Oh ask me not, bold sailor ;
Is not your ship a magic ship
That sails without a sail :
Are not these isles the Isles of Greece
And dust upon the sea ?
But answer me three questions
And give me answers three.
What is your ship ? "   " A British."
" And where may Britain be ? "
" Oh it lies north, dear lady ;
It is a small country."

173

" Yet you will know my lover
Though you live far away :
And you will whisper where he has gone,
That lily boy to look upon
And whiter than the spray."
" How should I know your lover,
Lady of the sea ? "
" Alexander, Alexander,
The King of the World was he."
" Weep not for him, dear lady,
But come aboard my ship.
So many years ago he died,
He's dead as dead can be."
" O base and brutal sailor
To lie this lie to me.
His mother was the foam-foot
Star-sparkling Aphrodite ;
His father was Adonis
Who lives away in Lebanon,
In stony Lebanon, where blooms
His red anemone.
But where is Alexander,
The soldier Alexander,
My golden love of olden days
The King of the world and me ? "

She sank into the moonlight
And the sea was only sea.

A Ship, an Isle, a Sickle Moon

A ship, an isle, a sickle moon—
With few but with how splendid stars
The mirrors of the sea are strewn
Between their silver bars !

＊　　＊　　＊

An isle beside an isle she lay,
The pale ship anchored in the bay,
While in the young moon's port of gold
A star-ship—as the mirrors told—
Put forth its great and lonely light
To the unreflecting Ocean, Night.
And still, a ship upon her seas,
The isle and the island cypresses
Went sailing on without the gale :
And still there moved the moon so pale,
A crescent ship without a sail !

Oak and Olive

I

Though I was born a Londoner,
  And bred in Gloucestershire,
I walked in Hellas years ago
  With friends in white attire :
And I remember how my soul
  Drank wine as pure as fire.

And when I stand by Charing Cross
  I can forget to hear
The crash of all those smoking wheels,
  When those cold flutes and clear
Pipe with such fury down the street,
  My hands grow moist with fear.

And there's a hall in Bloomsbury
  No more I dare to tread,
For all the stone men shout at me
  And swear they are not dead ;
And once I touched a broken girl
  And knew that marble bled.

II

But when I walk in Athens town
  That swims in dust and sun
Perverse, I think of London then
  Where massive work is done,
And with what sweep at Westminster
  The rayless waters run.

I ponder how from Attic seed
  There grew an English tree,
How Byron like his heroes fell,
  Fighting a country free,
And Swinburne took from Shelley's lips
  The kiss of Poetry.

And while our poets chanted Pan
  Back to his pipes and power,
Great Verrall, bending at his desk,
  And searching hour on hour
Found out old gardens, where the wise
  May pluck a Spartan flower.

III

When I go down the Gloucester lanes
  My friends are deaf and blind :
Fast as they turn their foolish eyes
  The Mænads leap behind,
And when I hear the fire-winged feet,
  They only hear the wind.

Have I not chased the fluting Pan
  Through Cranham's sober trees ?
Have I not sat on Painswick Hill
  With a nymph upon my knees,
And she as rosy as the dawn,
  And naked as the breeze ?

IV

But when I lie in Grecian fields,
  Smothered in asphodel,
Or climb the blue and barren hills,
  Or sing in woods that smell
With such hot spices of the South
  As mariners might sell—

Then my heart turns where no sun burns,
  To lands of glittering rain,
To fields beneath low-clouded skies
  New-widowed of their grain,
And Autumn leaves like blood and gold
  That strew a Gloucester lane.

V

Oh well I know sweet Hellas now,
  And well I knew it then,
When I with starry lads walked out—
  But ah, for home again !
Was I not bred in Gloucestershire,
  One of the Englishmen !

Brumana

Oh shall I never never be home again ?
Meadows of England shining in the rain
Spread wide your daisied lawns : your ramparts green
With briar fortify, with blossom screen
Till my far morning—and O streams that slow
And pure and deep through plains and playlands go,
For me your love and all your kingcups store,
And—dark militia of the southern shore,
Old fragrant friends—preserve me the last lines
Of that long saga which you sung me, pines,
When, lonely boy, beneath the chosen tree
I listened, with my eyes upon the sea.

O traitor pines, you sang what life has found
The falsest of fair tales.
Earth blew a far-horn prelude all around,
That native music of her forest home,
While from the sea's blue fields and syren dales
Shadows and light noon-spectres of the foam
Riding the summer gales
On aery viols plucked an idle sound.

Hearing you sing, O trees,
Hearing you murmur, " There are older seas,
That beat on vaster sands,
Where the wise snailfish move their pearly towers
To carven rocks and sculptured promont'ries,"
Hearing you whisper, " Lands
Where blaze the unimaginable flowers."

Beneath me in the valley waves the palm,
Beneath, beyond the valley, breaks the sea ;
Beneath me sleep in mist and light and calm
Cities of Lebanon, dream-shadow-dim,
Where Kings of Tyre and Kings of Tyre did rule
In ancient days in endless dynasty,
And all around the snowy mountains swim
Like mighty swans afloat in heaven's pool.

But I will walk upon the wooded hill
Where stands a grove, O pines, of sister pines,
And when the downy twilight droops her wing
And no sea glimmers and no mountain shines
My heart shall listen still.
For pines are gossip pines the wide world through
And full of runic tales to sigh or sing.
'Tis ever sweet through pines to see the sky
Mantling a deeper gold or darker blue.
'Tis ever sweet to lie
On the dry carpet of the needles brown,

And though the fanciful green lizard stir
And windy odours light as thistledown
Breathe from the lavdanon and lavender,
Half to forget the wandering and pain,
Half to remember days that have gone by,
And dream and dream that I am home again!

Areiya

This place was formed divine for love and us to dwell ;
This house of brown stone built for us to sleep therein ;
Those blossoms haunt the rocks that we should see and
smell ;
Those old rocks break the hill that we the heights should
win.

Those heights survey the sea that there our thoughts should
sail
Up the steep wall of wave to touch the Syrian sky :
For us that sky at eve fades out of purple pale,
Pale as the mountain mists beneath our house that lie.

In front of our small house are brown stone arches three ;
Behind it, the low porch where all the jasmine grows ;
Beyond it, red and green, the gay pomegranate tree ;
Around it, like love's arms, the summer and the rose.

Within it sat and wrote in minutes soft and few
This worst and best of songs, one who loves it, and you.

Bryan of Brittany

Roses are golden or white or red
  And green or grey for a sea,
But the loveliest girl alive, men said,
  Was Bryan of Brittany.

Court or courtier never a one
  Had Bryan the farmer's lass :
Her glorious hair was spread in the sun
  And her feet were dewed in the grass.

Evening opened a flower in the skies
  And shut the others asleep :
Home she came with the West in her eyes,
  Driving her silver sheep.

" O Mother, say, and brothers seven,
  What guests are these we have
With beards as white as the snow of heaven
  And their dark faces grave ?

" But are they merchants from the towns
  Or captains from the sea,
These that are clothed in crimson gowns,
  And bow to the earth to me ? "

183

"O kiss me, Bryan, and take the ring:
  Kiss me good-bye, my daughter:
You're to marry a crownèd king
  In Babylon over the water."

Golden hair as the gold of a rose
  Had Bryan of Brittany,
And her breasts were white as the foam, and the light
  Of her eyes was the light of the sea.

"What shall I do in Babylon
  A crownèd king to keep?
I'll not leave you and my brother John
  And my flock of silver sheep."

"Ah, Bryan, bravely spoken,
  And bravely, dear, you speak,
Not to leave me heart-broken
  And mother old and weak."

Said James the eldest brother,
  With his deep black eyes ablaze,
"They bring us gold, O mother,
  And jewels with red rays."

And John, the youngest brother,
  Whose eyes were bright and blue,
Said, "Let her go, my mother:
  I'll bring her back to you."

"Swear by Christ's love then, my son John,
    That when I feel the pain
You'll go to leafy Babylon
    And bring her back again."

"By Christ upon the Cross who bled
    And the seventy saints of Rome,
I'll go there living or go there dead,
    And bring my sister home."

II

It fell the mother had not seen
    A second Whitsuntide
Since Bryan sailed, a Persian Queen,
    When her seven sons all died.

"O false and faithless, my son John,
    And traitor in your tomb :
Who now will go to Babylon
    And bring me Bryan home ?—

"Whose hair is the golden gold of a rose,
    And red rose lips has she,
And her breasts are as white as the foam, and the light
    Of her eyes is the light of the sea."

185

III

It chanced a summer night so fair,
  A night so fair and calm,
Bryan was combing her beautiful hair
  In the moon, beneath a palm.

And gently sounded through the skies
  Slow bells of Babylon,
When there came one with bright blue eyes
  And the face of her brother John.

" Bryan, away from Babylon :
  Our mother weeps to-night ! "
" How tall you are, my brother John,
  And your blue eyes how bright ! "

" Oh, I am tall enough to stand
  And eyed enough to see,
And we'll go round by way of the land
  From here to Brittany."

Days went on and the road went on
  And skies brought paler skies :—
" You never sleep, my brother John,
  You never close your eyes."

" O Bryan, sister, do not fear,
  And Bryan, do not weep :
Before I came to find you, dear,
  I had enough of sleep."

Days went on and the road went on,
  And stars to pale or shine :—
" You never eat, my brother John,
  Nor drink a drop of wine."

" Fear not, dear girl : though long our road
  So great a strength is mine,
For I have eaten holy food,
  And drunk a scented wine."

A month and a year and a day had gone,
  They came to a sweet country :
O the silver shades of the forest glades
  Of Bryan's Brittany !

And the little birds began to talk
  In voices faintly human :—
" Who ever saw a dead man walk
  Beside a rosy woman ? "

" O brother, listen to the birds
  Chattering all together ! "
" The talk of the birds is feather words
  And lighter than a feather.

" Open, mother, to your son John,
  And open to your daughter :
I bring you Bryan from Babylon,
  From Babylon over the water.

" And her hair is the golden gold of a rose,
    And her lips as the red rose tree,
And her breasts are as white as the foam, and the light
    Of her eyes is the light of the sea.

" But I must back and over the hill,
    And Bryan must over the sea,
And you, old mother, who sit quite still,
    Must over the hill with me."

Don Juan Declaims

I am Don Juan, curst from age to age
By priestly tract and sentimental stage :
Branded a villain or believed a fool,
Battered by hatred, seared by ridicule,
Noble on earth, all but a king in Hell,
I am Don Juan with a tale to tell.
    Hot leapt the dawn from deep Plutonian fires
And ran like blood among the twinkling spires.
The market quickened : carts came rattling down :
Good human music roared about the town,
" And come," they cried, " and buy the best of Spain's
Great fireskinned fruits with cold and streaming veins !"
Others, " The man who'd make a lordly dish,
Would buy my speckled or my silver fish."
And some, " I stitch you raiment to the rule ! "
And some, " I sell you attar of Stamboul ! "
" And I have lapis for your love to wear,
Pearls for her neck and amber for her hair."
Death has its gleam. They swing before me still,
The shapes and sounds and colours of Seville !
    For there I learnt to love the plot, the fight,
The masker's cloak, the ladder set for flight,

The stern pursuit, the rapier's glint of death,
The scent of starlit roses, beauty's breath,
The music and the passion and the prize,
Aragon lips and Andalusian eyes.
This day a democrat I scoured the town ;
Courting, the next, I brought a princess down :
Now in some lady's panelled chamber hid
Achieved what love approves and laws forbid,
Now walked and whistled round the sleepy farms
And clasped a Dulcinea in my arms.
    I was the true, the grand idealist :
My light could pierce the pretty golden mist
That hides from common souls the starrier climes :
I loved as small men do ten-thousand times :
Rose to the blue triumphant, curved my bow,
Set high the mark and brought an angel low,
And laced with that brave body and shining soul
Learnt how to live, then learnt to love the whole.
And I first broke that jungle dark and dense,
Which hides the silver house of Commonsense,
And dissipated that disastrous lie
Which makes a god of stuffless Unity,
And drave the dark behind me, and revealed
A Pagan sunrise on a Christian field.
    My legend tells how once, by passion moved,
I slew the father of a girl I loved,
Then summoned—like an old and hardened sinner—
The brand-new statue of the dead to dinner.
My ribald guests, with Spanish wine aflame,
Were most delighted when the statue came,

Bowed to the party, made a little speech,
And bore me off beyond their human reach.
Well, priests must flourish and the truth must pale :
A very pious, entertaining tale.
   But this believe.   I struck a ringing blow
At sour Authority's ancestral show,
And stirred the sawdust understuffing all
The sceptred or the surpliced ritual.
I willed my happiness, kept bright and brave
My thoughts and deeds this side the accursed grave.
Life was a ten-course banquet after all,
And neatly rounded by my funeral.
" Pale guest, why strip the roses from your brow ?
" We hope to feast till morning." " Who knocks now ? "
" Twelve of the clock, Don Juan."   In came he,
That shining, tall and cold Authority,
Whose marble lips smile down on lips that pray,
And took my hand, and I was led away.

The Painter's Mistress

And still you paint, and still I stand
  White and erect, the classic pose,
And still, a soft-winged bee, your hand
  Moves comrade of a glance that flows
Over my body like love's tide :
And still the pale noon-shadows glide.

And still I hear each sound that falls,
  The wood that starts in the sun's heat,
The mouse astir among the walls,
  While down the summer-smitten street
A cart rolls lonely on : the hush
Tightens : I hear the flickering brush.

So with sweet pain for hour on hour
  I to your dark and roving eyes
Abandon more than Love had power
  To offer, in Love's mysteries :
You see me with the deeper sight,
Veiled in faint air and gemmed with light.

192

So shall the gaze of the soul-deep lover
  Guide where the sunray darts and swims
Down from the shoulders : still discover
  The rose and iris of these limbs,
Low flames that haunt the curve and fold
And in dark hollow tresses, gold.

In Hospital

Would I might lie like this, without the pain,
   For seven years—as one with snowy hair,
Who in the high tower dreams his dying reign—

   Lie here and watch the walls—how grey and bare,
The metal bed-post, the uncoloured screen,
   The mat, the jug, the cupboard, and the chair;

And served by an old woman, calm and clean,
   Her misted face familiar, yet unknown,
Who comes in silence, and departs unseen,

   And with no other visit, lie alone,
Nor stir, except I had my food to find
   In that dull bowl Diogenes might own.

And down my window I would draw the blind,
   And never look without, but, waiting, hear
A noise of rain, a whistling of the wind,

   And only know that flame-foot Spring is near
By trilling birds, or by the patch of sun
   Crouching behind my curtain. So, in fear,

Noon-dreams should enter, softly, one by one,
And throng about the floor, and float and play
And flicker on the screen, while minutes run—

The last majestic minutes of the day—
And with the mystic shadows, Shadow grow.
Then the grey square of wall should fade away,

And glow again, and open, and disclose
The shimmering lake in which the planets swim,
And all that lake a dewdrop on a rose.

Taoping

Across the vast blue-shadow-sweeping plain
The gathered armies darken through the grain,
Swinging curved swords and dragon-sculptured spears,
Footmen, and tiger-hearted cavaliers.
Them Government (whose fragrance Poets sing)
Hath bidden break the rebels of Taoping,
And fire and fell the monstrous fort of fools
Who dream that men may dare the deathless rules.
Such, grim example even now can show
Where high before the Van, in triple row,
First fiery blossom of rebellion's tree,
Twelve spear-stemmed heads are dripping silently.
(On evil day you sought, O ashen lips,
The kiss of women from our town of ships,
Nor ever dreamt, O spies, of falser spies,
The poppied cup and passion-mocking eyes !)

By these grim civil trophies undismayed,
In lacquered panoplies the chiefs parade.
Behind, the plain's floor rocks : the armies come :
The rose-round lips blow battle horns : the drum

Booms oriental measure. Earth exults.
And still behind, the tottering catapults
Pulled by slow slaves, grey backs with crimson lines,
Roll resolutely west. And still behind,
Down the canal's hibiscus-shaded marge
The glossy mules draw on the cedar barge,
Railed silver, blue-silk-curtained, which within
Bears the Commander, the old Mandarin,
Who never left his palace gates before,
But hath grown blind reading great books on war.

Now level on the land and cloudless red
The sun's slow circle dips toward the dead.
Night-hunted, all the monstrous flags are furled :
The Armies halt, and round them halts the World.
A phantom wind flies out among the rice ;
Hush turns the twin horizons in her vice ;
Air thickens : earth is pressed upon earth's core.
The cedar barge swings gently to the shore
Among her silver shadows and the swans :
The blind old man sets down his pipe of bronze.
The long whips cease. The slaves slacken the chain .
The gaunt-towered engines space the silent plain.
The hosts like men held in a frozen dream
Stiffen. The breastplates drink the scarlet gleam.
But the Twelve Heads with shining sockets stare
Further and further West. Have they seen there,
Black on blood's sea and huger than Death's wing,
Their *cannon-bowelled* fortress of Taoping ?

Virgil's Æneid, Book VI*

(ll. 1–19)

Tearful he spake : then drave the fleet along :
At length to Cumæ, by Eubœans raised,
They gliding came : set prows to face the sea,
Struck deep the anchor's stubborn tooth, festooned
Its harbour with the sweep of curved array.
Then leap the young ashore with flashing souls
(Are not the sands Hesperian ?) : they strike
Flints for their veins' hot secret, or they stray
With cleavesome axe unhoming furry beasts
Or shew on what tracks water may be found.
　　But this meanwhile god-fearing Æneas
Seeks the gapped cave where high Apollo reigns
And his dire Sybil murmurs truth of doom,
Mind and soul breathed on by the god-inspired
To flash out prophecies. They have come near
Diana's garden and her golden fane.
　　Dædalus once, Minoan realms to flee

* **Author's Note.**—I have of course tried to translate the sound
of the thing rather than the text—*cf.* my translation of "armatus,"
l. 388, and of "noctemque profundam," l. 462.

—Brave with great swooping wings to swim the sky
Steered a blind journey to the windy North
Till his strange shadows darkened Cumæ's rock.
He, there alighting, there to Earth returned,
To Phœbus sacrificed those oars, his wings.

*   *   *   *

(ll. 264–547)

Gods of the ghostly Empire and ye shades
So still, Chaos and Phlegethon so still
With leagues of night around you, me empower
Heard tales to tell : me with high aid empower
Earth's deep-embowelled secret to betray !
    They went obscure in lowering lone night
Through lodges of King Dis, untenanted,—
Featureless lands. Thus goes a forest pathway
Beneath the curst light of the wav'ring moon,
When Jove has gloomed the sky, and pitchy dark
Uncoloured all the world. In Hell's first reach
Fronting the very vestibule of Orcus
Griefs and the Cares have set their couches down,—
The vengeful Cares. There pale Diseases dwell,
Sad Eld and Fear and loathsome Poverty
And Hunger, that bad counsellor,—dire shapes—
And Death and Toil, and Sleep brother of Death
And soul-corrupting joys. Opposed he viewed
War the great murderer, and those steel bowers
The Furies deck for bridal, and Discord
Daft, with blood-ribbons on her serpent hair.
    But straight in front a huge black knotted elm

Stood branching : here, they say, the Vain Dreams roost ;—
There's not a leaf without one stuck behind!
Next he saw twisted beasts of the old tales :
Centaurs were stabled at the gates : Scyllas
Spread their twin shapes, Briareus his hundred arms.
And Lerna's beast behold hissing out fear,
Chimæra too, who fights with fire, and Gorgons
And Harpies, and a shade with a triple form !
Such was the horror seized Æneas then
He made to meet their onset with cold steel,
And had th' instructed Sybil not advised
That these were gossamer vitalities
Flitting in stuffless mockery of form,
He'd have leapt on and lashed the empty air.
    Hence leads a road to Acheron, vast flood
Of thick and restless slime : all that foul ooze
It belches in Cocytus. Here keeps watch
That wild and filthy pilot of the marsh
Charon, from whose rugged old chin trails down
The hoary beard of centuries : his eyes
Are fixed, but flame. His grimy cloak hangs loose
Rough-knotted at the shoulder : his own hands
Pole on the boat, or tend the sail that wafts
His dismal skiff and its fell freight along.
Ah, he is old, but with that toughening eld
That speaks his godhead ! To the bank and him
All a great multitude came pouring down,
Brothers and husbands, and the proud-souled heroes.
Life's labour done : and boys and unwed maidens
And the young men by whose flame-funeral

Parents had wept. - Many as leaves that fall
Gently in autumn when the sharp cold comes
Or all the birds that flock at the turn o' the year
Over the ocean to the lands of light.
They stood and prayed each one to be first taken :
They stretched their hands for love of the other side,
But the grim sailor takes now these, now those :
And some he drives a distance from the shore.
Æneas, moved and marvelling at this stir
Cried—" O chaste Sibyl tell me why this throng
That rushes to the river ?   What desire
Have all these phantoms ? and what rule's award
Drives these back from the marge, let those go over
Sweeping the livid shallows with the oar ? "
The old priestess replied in a few words,
" Son of Anchises of true blood divine,
Behold the deep Cocytus and dim Styx
By whom the high gods fear to swear in vain.
This shiftless crowd all is unsepulchred :
The boatman there is Charon : those who embark
The buried.   None may leave this beach of horror
To cross the growling stream before that hour
That hides their white bones in a quiet tomb.
A hundred years they flutter round these shores :
Then they may cross the waters long desired."
    Æneas stopped and stood there heavily
Thoughtful and sad for this unfair decree.
Wretched for lack of sepulchre he saw
Leucaspis and the Lycian convoy's chief
Orontes.   They left Troy with rough sea

And lost their ships and crew to the south-west wind.
There too did roam the pilot Palinurus,
Who steering up from Libya by the stars
Had fallen from the stern a few days since
Deep in the wave.   So girt with gloom stood he
The hero scarce could see—but seeing, he cried :—
" Thee, Palinurus, what relentless god
Tore from our love to drown thee in mid main ?
Say, for Apollo never yet found false
Deceived me here, in mystic song foretelling
That safe across the waters thou shouldst come
To tread Italian soil.   Is this kept promise ? "
But he :—" Captain, the Tripod sang no lies
Nor was't a god that flung me to the waves,
But whilst I steered, the chance of a sharp shock
So wrenched the gear entrusted to my hands
That clinging fast I was swept overboard
Tiller and all.   Witness, O passionate waves,
Less did I fear my peril than the ship's
Which now dismantled and its pilot gone
Rode at the mercy of the bristling swell.
Three winter nights across the infinite sea
The strong South bore me, piling up the waves ;
But the fourth morning from a billow's crest
I saw the cliffs of Italy and swam
Landwards slowly.   For now was danger past
Had not a cruel folk come on with swords,
As weighted by my dripping clothes I clutched
A broken rock's summit with crooked hand,
And deemed me—brutes—a prize.   Sport of the waves

Is Palinurus now, and the winds whirl him
All up and down the shore.   By the kind light
And spacious air I pray thee : by thy Sire
And young Iulus growing fair and tall
Defeat my woes, unconquerable man !
Either cast earth upon me—as thou mayst
To Veline harbour steering, or maybe
If there's a way—thy mother was divine
And much it needeth the god's help to float
On such grand rivers and the Stygian mere—
Hold out thy hand to one who is in sorrow,
Bear me across the wave !   So shall I know
At least of Death the quiet and the home."
He spake : the Sibyl answered : " Palinurus
What dread desire is thine ?   Wouldst thou attempt,
Unburied, waves of Styx and that stern stream
The Furies haunt ?   Wouldst thou approach that shore
And have no mandate ?   Dost thou hope to melt
Fate with a prayer ?   But listen and take heart
For all the people of the cities round
Driven forth by omens dire from the high heaven
Shall honour thy remains and raise a tomb
And on thy tomb shall all due rites perform
And all that place for evermore shall keep
The name of Palinurus."   As she spake
His trouble ceased : a while from his sad heart
Grief flies.   He is glad the land should bear his name.
   Set path pursuing they approached the stream
Whom soon the sailor of the Stygian wave
Saw pass the silent wood and seek the marge

And hailed censorious :—" Thou who walkest down
Clashing thy armour by our streams of Hell,
Speak thy intent : there on thy road stand still !
Here lies the land of shadow dream and night,
And no warm flesh may ride on Stygian keel.
Small joy had I admitting to this mere
Hercules or those victor sons of Heaven
Peirithoos and Theseus.   Hercules
Chained with bare hands the dog of Tartarus
And dragged him from the throne quaking : they came
To rape our mistress from the bed of Dis."
" We spin no snares," the Amphrysian sharp replied :
" Be soothed, no violence these arms portend.
Let the huge Janitor's eternal cry
Still from his cave confound the bloodless ghosts,
And Proserpine unravished still attend
Her kinsman's threshold.   Æneas of Troy,
Famed dutiful and fearless, here descends
To embrace his father in your pits of gloom.
If high devotion spells thee nought, this bough
(She drew it from her breast) may move thee still."
    Calm sank the heart but now swoln out with rage :
With no word more, eyeing that ancient bough,
Doom's symbol, after ages seen again,
Turned he his cærule prow and made the shore.
Thence other souls who sat along the dunes
He drave, and let his gangway down, and took
The huge Æneas in his patchèd punt,
Which groaned o'ercargoed ; and through many a crack
Oozed up the mere : yet safe across the stream

Sybil and soldier did he row, and beached
On the green formless slime of the other side.
   Cerberus here sends ringing through his realm
A triple-throated howling, couched, immune,
With cavern for a kennel. The Priestess,
Seeing his dragon necks stiffen to strike,
A cake of honey and bemusing herbs
Tossed him. Three maws the ravening monster spread,
Snapped it in air, and all his hugesome bulk
Uncoiled and sprawled and stretched across the cave.
Æneas down the brute-unwardened path
Quick pace pursues. Behind him lies the stream
Whose waves whisper no whisper of return.
   Now cries are heard, and thin abundant wind :
All down Hell's forecourt weep the Infant Souls,
Whom shareless of life's shining dower, Doom
Tore from the breast and whelmed in Death's sharp wave,
Near, men judged out of life by false decree.
They have their urn, their Umpire, these abodes :
'Tis Minos draws the lots, he who may call
The council of the silent : he who reads,
Grand arbiter, the histories of men.
And next them flit the Sad Ones who prepared
With their rash hands their own extinction's cup
And flung their souls on dark to spite the day.
Ah could they, could they back to the bright sky
What years would they not bear of toil or pain !
Law bars them fast : the mere's grim loveless wave
Bounds their domain : Styx nine times interfused
Imprisons. Here the Broken-hearted Fields

Roll out to the horizon. Such their name.
Here those whom Love remorseless and unkind
Devoured by dissolution, walk in peace
Down secret byways of a myrtle forest.
Here Phædra, Procris and sad Eriphyle
He saw, whom her fierce son had wounded sore,
Pasiphæ, Evadne : in their train
Laodamia, and that once a boy
Now woman, Cæneus, thus reshaped by doom.
Among them one love-pierced not long ago,—
Dido of Carthage roamed the tall grove through
Whom when Troy's hero drawing near beheld
Gliding through murk and shadow, as one sees
Or dreams to see through clouds the thin new moon,
He wept, calling her with a lover's cry :—
" Dido ill-starred, but was it truth they told me,
Thy fate—the self-sought ending by the sword ?
To death I brought thee. O by the stars I swear
By the high gods and by all faith that holds
In Earth's black core, unwilling, O my queen,
Sailed I away from Carthage. But the gods
They who now send me through this shadow world,
These lands so far, this oceanic night,
Drave me with uncharitable command
Nor could I dream sorrow as sharp as that
Should wait on my departure. But stay, stay !
I do not pass so soon : whom dost thou flee ?
Fate grants me thus to hail thee the last time ! "
So tried Æneas through his tears to assuage
That shy wild spirit glancing round in fear :

But she looked down, turning her face aside,
A face as unresponsive to appeal
As a hard flint or a high marble mountain.
Then darting back, down the dark grove she flies
Unfriendly, where Sichæus, her old spouse,
His gentleness love's proxy, tends her still.
Æneas, victim of a chance unfair
Still follows, weeps, and pities as she flies.
    But now, their journey's settled path pursuing,
On to the ultimate secret fields they move,
Where walk the mighty Captains. Tydeus here
He saw, and Parthenopæus, warrior bold,
And one that seemed Adrastus, and so pale,
And all the war-mown Trojans, for whose fate
Such tears had been shed in the face of heaven.
Rank upon rank he, sorrowful, saw them,—
Glaucus and Medon and Thersilochus,
Antenor's son and Polyphœtes, vowed
Demeter's, and still armed, still charioted
Idæus.   Right and left the Spirits crowd
To their eyes' festival, to dally pleased,
Or step beside, or ask him all his tale.
But when the Danaan phalanx and great hosts
Of Agamemnon saw a Man and Arms
That flashed among the shadows, terrible fear
Set them aquiver : as to the ships of old
Some turned to flee : some raised a little cry,
So thin its echoes mocked their gaping mouths.
    Here saw he Priam's son, Deiphobus,
With all his body rent, all his face torn

And both his hands, and ravaged earless head,
And cut nostrils—dishonourable wounds.
Yet could he recognize the quaking ghost
That strove to veil the horror of its face
And called him in the voice he could well know :—
" Deiphobus, Hero of old Trojan blood,
Who willed you this vile punishment ? To whom
Was power against you given. Rumour told me
On that last night how on a tower of dead,
Weary with slaughter of the Greeks, you lay
Prone. It was I then raised on Rhætian shore
The empty mound and thrice with a loud cry
Summoned thy wraith. Arms and a name preserve
That place—but thee, dear friend, I could not find
To bury e'er I left my native land."
But Priam's son :—" Friend, what couldst thou do more ?
Thou hast paid every due to death and me.
But me my destiny true the sin
Of that She-murderess of Spartan brood
Whelmed in these woes : these are her monuments.
How in deceitful pleasure that last night
We spent, well dost thou know, too well must know,—
When with a leap o'er steep-stoned Pergamon
Pregnant with soldiery, the fatal horse
Its bristling burden flung. She, she it was
With traitor dance led round our Phrygian dames
The wild Evoe proclaiming ! A huge torch
She shook above the revel, which did call
The Danaans from Troy Tower. I heavily
Slept the meanwhile on couch of doom, and me

Deep honied quiet, miming Death's own peace,
Thralled.   And my dear spouse, busy all the while,
Strips the house bare of arms : and my good sword 's
No longer at my pillow.   ' Ready now !
In Menelaus !   Every door's ajar ! '
This was her great gift to her old lover,
And this her scheme for hushing up old tales !
Quick to the end now !   They break in my door,
With them Ulysses, Crime's High Advocate.
Gods, load this on the Greeks,—if the good man
Who cries down vengeance be a good man still !
But thee alive what hap—tell in thy turn—
Brought here ?   Dost come a plaything of the wave
By traveller's chance ?   Or at the hest divine ?
What fate's oppression draws thee to these homes
Where no sun shines nor any view stands clear ? "
    But while they talked, across the pole of heaven
Had swept the Charioteer who drives from Dawn,
And dalliance had soon eaten up the dole
Of time allotted : so the Sybil warned—
" Down comes the night, Æneas : all too fast
We weep the hours away.   Here splits the road,
Right, to the foot of the big walls of Dis,
But the left leads the damned to their deserts
In impious Tartary."   " But chide no more,"
Replied Deiphobus : " I will return :
My place is in the roll-call of the Dead,
Go, Splendour of our Story : grace be thine
Beyond our measure."   And he turned away.

The Dying Patriot

Day breaks on England down the Kentish hills,
Singing in the silence of the meadow-footing rills,
Day of my dreams, O day !
  I saw them march from Dover, long ago,
  With a silver cross before them, singing low,
Monks of Rome from their home where the blue seas break
    in foam,
  Augustine with his feet of snow.

Noon strikes on England, noon on Oxford town,
—Beauty she was statue cold—there's blood upon her gown :
Noon of my dreams, O noon !
  Proud and godly kings had built her, long ago,
  With her towers and tombs and statues all arow,
With her fair and floral air and the love that lingers there,
  And the streets where the great men go.

Evening on the olden, the golden sea of Wales,
When the first star shivers and the last wave pales :
O evening dreams !

There's a house that Britons walked in, long ago,
Where now the springs of ocean fall and flow,
And the dead robed in red and sea-lilies overhead
Sway when the long winds blow.

Sleep not, my country : though night is here, afar
Your children of the morning are clamorous for war :
Fire in the night, O dreams !
  Though she send you as she sent you, long ago,
  South to desert, east to ocean, west to snow,
West of these out to seas colder than the Hebrides
    I must go
  Where the fleet of stars is anchored and the young
    Star-captains glow.

A Sacred Dialogue

(*Christmas* 1912)

The silver Bishop of Bethlehem,
A desolate Turkish town,
Speaks with a shape each Christmas day
That floats to music down.

THE BISHOP OF BETHLEHEM

Peace and goodwill, Son of the King!
Thy Birthday and Thy Star!

CHRIST

Peace and goodwill the world may sing:
But we shall talk of war!

How fare my armies of the North?

212

THE BISHOP

They wait victorious peace,
All the high forts of Macedon
Fly the proud flag of Greece.

CHRIST

Then surely on that Eastern dome
The Allies' cross is gleaming,
Redeemed my loved and ancient home! *

THE BISHOP

Ah, it still waits redeeming!

CHRIST

Still waits—Five hundred years, and still
My soldiers wait—so long?

THE BISHOP

Thou hast Fate's sceptre.   What thy will
Dooms could split earth, thou Strong!

* St. Sophia.

213

CHRIST

My nations are steel towers built tall,
  Shepherd of Bethlehem,
Tell none this Moslem cracked stone wall
  Is more than jest for them ?

Yet Islam oft would strip and slay
  Christian woman and child,
And Europe feast that Christmas day
  A coward reconciled.

Yet some day o'er Pamphylian waves
  Shall Byzant chants be ringing,
And rose-crowned hermits leave their caves
  And sail to Patmos singing ;

Some day Nicea's pool again
  Shall bear the creed of the World,
And that day crashing from my fane
  Shall that horned moon be hurled.

Then some deep-faithed Priest will shout :
  Oh, cease ye bells forlorn,
We have forgotten Jerusalem
  And the land where He was born ! "

Then the black cannons of the Lord
   Shall wake crusading ghosts
And the Milky Way shall swing like a sword
When Jerusalem vomits its horde
On the Christmas day preferred of the Lord,
   The Christmas day of the Hosts !

Note by the Author.—Originally written for Christmas 1912, and referring to the first Balkan War, this poem contains in the last speech of Christ words that ring like a prophecy of events that may occur very soon.

December 1914

The Old Ships

I have seen old ships sail like swans asleep
Beyond the village which men still call Tyre,
With leaden age o'ercargoed, dipping deep
For Famagusta and the hidden sun
That rings black Cyprus with a lake of fire;
And all those ships were certainly so old
Who knows how oft with squat and noisy gun,
Questing brown slaves or Syrian oranges,
The pirate Genoese
Hell-raked them till they rolled
Blood, water, fruit and corpses up the hold.
But now through friendly seas they softly run,
Painted the mid-sea blue or shore-sea green,
Still patterned with the vine and grapes in gold.

But I have seen,
Pointing her shapely shadows from the dawn
And image tumbled on a rose-swept bay,
A drowsy ship of some yet older day;
And, wonder's breath indrawn,

Thought I—who knows—who knows—but in that same
(Fished up beyond Ææa, patched up new
—Stern painted brighter blue—)
That talkative, bald-headed seaman came
(Twelve patient comrades sweating at the oar)
From Troy's doom-crimson shore,
And with great lies about his wooden horse
Set the crew laughing, and forgot his course.

It was so old a ship—who knows, who knows ?
—And yet so beautiful, I watched in vain
To see the mast burst open with a rose,
And the whole deck put on its leaves again.

The Blue Noon

When the whole sky is vestured silken blue
With not one fleece to view,
Drown your deep eyes afar, and see you must
How the light azure dust
And speckled atoms of the polished skies
Are large blue butterflies.
The proof ?   Lie in a field on heavy noons,
When Nature drones and croons
And on man's distant cry or dog's far bark
Hush sets the instant mark,
Look up : when nothing earthly stirs or sings
You hear them wave their wings,
And watch the breeze their vanity awakes
Light on the heavenly lakes.
But when the shades before the sun's huge fall
In sham retreat grow tall,
Their ambushed allies, the impatient stars,
Make ready for bright wars,
And shoot ten million arrows to chastise
The tardy butterflies
Who dive in hosts toward the diving sphere
That holds the light's frontier,
And the poor vanquished, turning as they glide,
Show their gold underside.

A Fragment

O pouring westering streams
Shouting that I have leapt the mountain bar,
Down curve on curve my journey's white way gleams—
My road along the river of return.

I know the countries where the white moons burn,
And heavy star on star
Dips on the pale and crystal desert hills.
I know the river of the sun that fills
With founts of gold the lakes of Orient sky.

·   ·   ·

And I have heard a voice of broken seas
And from the cliffs a cry.
Ah still they learn, those cave-eared Cyclades,
The Triton's friendly or his fearful horn
And why the deep sea-bells but seldom chime,
And how those waves and with what spell-swept rhyme
In years of morning, on a summer's morn

Whispering round his castle on the coast,
Lured young Achilles from his haunted sleep
And drave him out to dive beyond those deep
Dim purple windows of the empty swell,
His ivory body flitting like a ghost
Over the holes where flat blind fishes dwell,
All to embrace his mother thronèd in her shell.

Narcissus

O pool in which we dallied
　And splashed the prostrate Noon!
O Water-boy, more pallid
　Than any watery moon!
O Lilies round him turning!
　O broken Lilies, strewn!
O silver Lutes of Morning!
　O Red of the Drums of Noon!

O dusky-plumaged sorrow!
　O ebon Swans of Care—
I sought thee on the Morrow,
　And never found thee there!
I breathed the vapour-blended
　Cloud of a dim despair :
White lily, is it ended ?
　Gold lily—oh, golden hair!

The pool that was thy dwelling
　I hardly knew again,
So black it was, and swelling
　With bitter wind and rain.

'Mid the bowed leaves 1 lingered,
  Lashed by the blast of Pain,
Till evening, storm-rose-fingered,
  Beckoned to night again.

There burst a flood of Quiet
  Over the unstellèd skies ;
Full moon flashed out a-riot :
  Near her I dreamt thine eyes
Afloat with night, still trembling
  With captured mysteries :
But sulphured wracks, assembling,
  Redarkened the bright skies.

Ah, thou at least art lying
  Safe at the white nymph's feet,
Listless, while I, slow-dying,
  Twist my gaunt limbs for heat !
Yet I'll to Earth, my Mother :
  So, boy, I'll still entreat
Forgive me—for none other
  Like Earth is honey-sweet !

(See former version, page 30*)*

Stillness

When the words rustle no more,
  And the last work's done,
When the bolt lies deep in the door,
  And Fire, our Sun,
Falls on the dark-laned meadows of the floor;

When from the clock's last chime to the next chime
  Silence beats his drum,
And Space with gaunt grey eyes and her brother Time
  Wheeling and whispering come,
She with the mould of form and he with the loom of
  rhyme:

Then twittering out in the night my thought-birds flee,
  I am emptied of all my dreams:
I only hear Earth turning, only see
  Ether's long bankless streams,
And only know I should drown if you laid not your
  hand on me.

The Pensive Prisoner

My thoughts came drifting down the Prison where I lay—
Through the Windows of their Wings the stars were
    shining—
The wings bore me away—the russet Wings and grey
With feathers like the moon-bleached Flowers—I was a
    God reclining :
Beneath me lay my Body's Chain and all the Dragons born
    of Pain
As I burned through the Prison Roof to walk on Pavement
    Shining.

The Wild Wind of Liberty swept through my Hair and sang
    beyond :
I heard the Souls of men asleep chattering in the Eaves
And rode on topmost Boughs of Heaven's single-moon-
    fruited Silver Wand,
Night's unifying Tree whereof the central Stars be leaves—
O Thoughts, Thoughts, Thoughts,—Fire-angel-birds relent-
    less—
Will you not brood in God's Star-tree and leave Red Heart
    tormentless !

Hexameters

O happy Dome so lightly swimming through storm-riven
    Æther, .
Blue burning and gold, the hollow of Chaos adorning,
Shine, happy Dome of th' air, on Sea thy sister, on ancient
Plains, on sharp snowbeard mountains, on silvery waters,
On knotted eld-mossed trees, on roses starry with April—
But most shine upon one lying tormented, a dreamer,
Thy lover. Ah wherefore did a rift so cruel across thee
Open ? A long tremulous sighing comes thence, with a
    great wind,
Darkness ever blowing round thy blue curtain. A finger
Out of Hell aims at me. Gather, O sweet Dome o' the
    Morning,
Thy rapid ardent flamy quiver, thy splintery clusters :
Send a volley straight through to the heart of this desolation,
And burning, blasting with a shaft of thunderous azure,
Break the ebon soldiers, restore his realm to the dreamer !

Philomel

(*From the French of Paul Fort*)

O sing, in heart of silence hiding near,
Thou whom the roses bend their heads to hear !
In silence down the moonlight slides her wing :
Will no rose breathe while Philomel doth sing ?
No breath—and deeper yet the perfume grows :
The voice of Philomel can slay a rose :
The song of Philomel on nights serene
Implores the gods who roam in shades unseen,
But never calls the roses, whose perfume
Deepens and deepens, as they wait their doom.
Is it not silence whose great bosom heaves ?
Listen, a rose-tree drops her quiet leaves.

Now silence flashes lightning like a storm :
Now silence is a cloud, and cradled warm
By risings and by fallings of the tune
That Philomel doth sing, as shines the moon,
—A bird's or some immortal voice from Hell ?
There is no breath to die with, Philomel !

And yet the world has changed without a breath.
The moon lies heavy on the roses' death,
And every rosebush droops its leafy crown.
A gust of roses has gone sweeping down.

The panicked garden drives her leaves about :
The moon is masked : it flares and flickers out.
O shivering petals on your lawn of fear,
Turn down to Earth and hear what you shall hear.
A beat, a beat, a beat beneath the ground,
And hurrying beats, and one great beat profound.
A heart is coming close : I have heard pass
The noise of a great Heart upon the grass.
The petals reel.   Earth opens : from beneath
The ashen roses on their lawn of death,
Raising her peaceful brow, the grand and pale
Demeter listens to the nightingale.

From Jean Moréas' " Stances "

The garden rose I paid no honour to,
So humbly poised and fashioned on its spray,
Has now by wind unkissed, undrenched by dew,
Lived captive in her vase beyond a day.

And tired and pale, bereft of earth and sun,
Her blossom over and her hour of pride,
She has dropped all her petals, one by one,
Unmindful if she lived or how she died.

When doom is passing in her dusky glade
Let us learn silence.   In this evening hour,
O heart bowed down with mystery and shade,
Too heavy lies the spectre of a flower !

The Princess

(A Story from the Modern Greek)

A Princess armed a privateer to sail the Chersonese
And fitted it with purple sails to belly in the breeze,
With golden cords and oaken boards and a name writ
    out in pearls,
And all the jolly mariners were gallant little girls.

The King's Son he came hunting her in frigates two or three,
" Give me one kiss, Princess," he cried, " and take a ship
    from me ;
And would you like the yellow boat or would you like the
    red,
Or would you take myself and mine, the gold and green
    instead ? "

" Sir, handsome fellow as you are, it's curious, you know,
To ask a maid for kisses in mid-archipelago :
But come and fight with us, young man ; the prize is for
    the brave."
They fought : it chanced the lady won and took him for
    a slave.

She drave him to the yellow boat and lashed him to the oar.
" Now pull, my handsome Prince," said she, " till you can
pull no more."
" O Princess, do but listen to a valiant boy's appeal,
And take me from this bitter oar, and put me at the wheel."

" O foolish Prince," she answered him ; " back to your
oar and pull.
Row hard and soon we'll anchor in the gulf of Istamboul.
While the slaves collect provisions and the sailors go for
drink
You may chance to find your Captain not so brutal as you
think ! "

Pannyra of the Golden Heel

(From Albert Samain)

The revel pauses and the room is still :
The silver flute invites her with a trill,
And, buried in her great veils fold on fold,
Rises to dance Pannyra, Heel of Gold.
Her light steps cross ; her subtle arm impels
The clinging drapery ; it shrinks and swells,
Hollows and floats, and bursts into a whirl :
She is a flower, a moth, a flaming girl.
All lips are silent ; eyes are all in trance :
She slowly wakes the madness of the dance,
Windy and wild the golden torches burn ;
She turns, and swifter yet she tries to turn,
Then stops : a sudden marble stiff she stands.
The veil that round her coiled its spiral bands,
Checked in its course, brings all its folds to rest,
And clinging to bright limb and pointed breast
Shows, as beneath silk waters woven fine,
Pannyra naked in a flash divine !

The Gate of the Armies

(From Henri de Regnier)

Swing out thy doors, high gate that dreadst not night,
Bronze to the left and iron to the right.
Deep in a cistern has been flung thy key ;
If dread thee close, anathema on thee ;
And like twin shears let thy twin portals cut
The hand's fist through that would thee falsely shut
Again thy dusky vault hath heard resound
Steps of strong men who never yet gave ground,
Marching with whom came breathless and came bold
Victory naked with broad wings of gold.
Her glaive to guide them calmly soars and dips ;
Her kiss is lifeblood's purple on their lips.
From rose-round mouths the clarions shake and shrill,
A brazen boom of bees that hunt to kill.
" Drink, swarm of war, stream from your plated hives
And cull death's dust on flowery-fleshed fierce lives,
So, when back home to native town ye march,
Beneath those golden wings and my black arch
May all men watch my pavement, as each pace
Of your red feet leaves clear its sanguine trace."

November Eves

November Evenings! Damp and still
They used to cloak Leckhampton hill,
And lie down close on the grey plain,
And dim the dripping window-pane,
And send queer winds like Harlequins
That seized our elms for violins
And struck a note so sharp and low
Even a child could feel the woe.

Now fire chased shadow round the room;
Tables and chairs grew vast in gloom:
We crept about like mice, while Nurse
Sat mending, solemn as a hearse,
And even our unlearned eyes
Half closed with choking memories.

Is it the mist or the dead leaves,
Or the dead men—November eves?

God Save the King

God save our gracious King,
Nation and State and King,
   God save the King!
Grant him the Peace divine,
But if his Wars be Thine
Flash on our fighting line
   Victory's Wing!

Thou in his suppliant hands
Hast placed such Mighty Lands :
   Save thou our King!
As once from golden Skies
Rebels with flaming eyes,
So the King's Enemies
   Doom Thou and fling!

Mountains that break the night
Holds He by eagle right
   Stretching far Wing!
Dawn lands for Youth to reap,
Dim lands where Empires sleep,
His!   And the Lion Deep
   Roars for the King.

But most these few dear miles
Of sweetly-meadowed Isles,—
        England all Spring ;
Scotland that by the marge
Where the blank North doth charge
Hears Thy Voice loud and large,
        Save, and their King !

Grace on the golden Dales
Of Thine old Christian Wales
        Shower till they sing,
Till Erin's Island lawn
Echoes the dulcet-drawn
Song with a cry of Dawn—
        God save the King !

The Burial in England

These then we honour : these in fragrant earth
Of their own country in great peace forget
Death's lion-roar and gust of nostril-flame
Breathing souls across to the Evening Shore.
Soon over these the flowers of our hill-sides
Shall wake and wave and nod beneath the bee
And whisper love to Zephyr year on year,
Till the red war gleam like a dim red rose
Lost in the garden of the Sons of Time.
But ah what thousands no such friendly doom
Awaits,—whom silent comrades in full night
Gazing right and left shall bury swiftly
By the cold flicker of an alien moon.
    Ye veilèd women, ye with folded hands,
Mourning those you half hoped for Death too dear,
I claim no heed of you.   Broader than earth
Love stands eclipsing nations with his wings,
While Pain, his shadow, delves as black and deep
As he e'er flamed or flew.   Citizens draw
Back from their dead awhile.   Salute the flag !
    If this flag though royally always borne,
Deceived not dastard, ever served base gold ;

If the dark children of the old Forest
Once feared it, or ill Sultans mocked it furled,
Yet now as on a thousand death-reaped days
It takes once more the unquestionable road.
O bright with blood of heroes, not a star
Of all the north shines purer on the sea !
    Our foes—the hardest men a state can forge,
An army wrenched and hammered like a blade
Toledo-wrought neither to break nor bend,
Dipped in that ice the pedantry of power,
And toughened with wry gospels of dismay ;
Such are these who brake down the door of France,
Wolves worrying at the old World's honour,
Hunting Peace not to prison but her tomb.
But ever as some brown song-bird whose torn nest
Gapes robbery, darts on the hawk like fire,
So Peace hath answered, angry and in arms.
And from each grey hamlet and bright town of France
From where the apple or the olive grows
Or thin tall strings of poplars on the plains,
From the rough castle of the central hills,
From the three coasts—of mist and storm and sun,
And meadows of the four deep-rolling streams,
From every house whose windows hear God's bell
Crowding the twilight with the wings of prayer
And flash their answer in a golden haze,
Stream the young soldiers who are never tired.
For all the foul mists vanished when that land
Called clear, as in the sunny Alpine morn
The jodeler awakes the frosty slopes

To thunderous replies,—soon fading far
Among the vales like songs of dead children.
But the French guns' answer, ne'er to echoes weak
Diminished, bursts from the deep trenches yet ;
And its least light vibration blew to dust
The weary factions,—priest's or guild's or king's,
And side by side troop up the old partisans,
The same laughing, invincible, tough men
Who gave Napoleon Europe like a loaf,
For slice and portion,—not so long ago !
Either to Alsace or loved lost Lorraine
They pass, or inexpugnable Verdun
Ceintured with steel, or stung with faith's old cry
Assume God's vengeance for his temple stones.
But you maybe best wish them for the north
Beside you 'neath low skies in loamèd fields,
Or where the great line hard on the duned shore
Ends and night leaps to England's sea-borne flame.
Never one drop of Lethe's stagnant cup
Dare dim the fountains of the Marne and Aisne
Since still the flowers and meadow-grass unmown
Lie broken with the imprint of those who fell,
Briton and Gaul—but fell immortal friends
And fell victorious and like tall trees fell.

But young men, you who loiter in the town,
Need you be roused with overshouted words,
Country, Empire, Honour, Liége, Louvain ?
Pay your own Youth the duty of her dreams.
For what sleep shall keep her from the thrill
Of War's star-smiting music, with its swell

Of shore and forest and horns high in the wind,
 Yet pierced with that too sharp piping which if man
Hear and not fear he shall face God unscathed) ?
What, are you poets whose vain souls contrive
Sorties and sieges spun of the trickling moon
And such a rousing ghost-catastrophe
You need no concrete marvels to be saved ?
Or live you here too lustily for change ?
Sail you such pirate seas on such high quests,
Hunt you thick gold or striped and spotted beasts,
Or tread the lone ways of the swan-like mountains ?
Excused.   But if, as I think, breeched in blue,
Stalled at a counter, cramped upon a desk,
You drive a woman's pencraft—or a slave's,
What chain shall hold you when the trumpets play,
Calling from the blue hill behind your town,
Calling over the seas, calling for you !
" But "—do you murmur ?—" we'd not be as those.
Death is a dour recruiting-sergeant : see,
These women weep, we celebrate the dead."
Boys, drink the cup of warning dry.   Face square
That old grim hazard, " Glory-or-the-Grave."
Not we shall trick your pleasant years away,
Yet is not Death the great adventure still,
And is it all loss to set ship clean anew
When heart is young and life an eagle poised ?
Choose, you're no cowards.   After all, think some,
Since we are men and shrine immortal souls
Surely for us as for these nobly dead
The Kings of England lifting up their swords
Shall gather at the gate of Paradise.

The True Paradise

Lord, is the Poet to destruction vowed,
Like the dawn-feather of an April cloud,
Which signs in russet character or grey
The name of Beauty on the book of Day ?
We poets crave no heav'n but what is ours—
These trees beside these rivers ; these same flowers
Shaped and enfragranced to the English field
Where Thy best florist-craft is full revealed.
Trees by the river, birds upon the bough
My soul shall ask for, whose flesh enjoys them now
Through both the pale-blue windows of quick Mind ;
Grant me earth's treats in Paradise to find.
Nor listen to that island-bound St. John
Who'd have no Sea in Heaven, no Sea to sail upon !
Remake this World less Man's and Nature's Pain ;
Save such dear torment as the chill of Rain
When the sun flouts us like a maid her man
Drowned in long meshes of a silver Fan.
Nor, Lord, the good fatigue of labouring breath
Destroy, but only Sickness, Age and Death.
Let old Plays teach Despair's sad grandeur still
And legends trumpet War's last Hero-thrill.

So I and all my friends, still young, still wise,
Will shout along thy streets—" O Paradise ! "
But if prepared for me new Mansions are,
Chill and unknown, in some bright windy Star,
Mid strange-shaped Souls from all the Planets seven,
Lord, I fear deep, and would not go to Heaven.
Rather in feather-mist I'd fade away
Like the Dawn-writing of an April day.

Ode to the Glory of Greece

(*A Fragment*)

Hellas victorious !
Two came to me at night
Glorious
With that Elysian light
Which round the phantoms of great Poets dead
Hovers, as once in their blue earthly eyes
Played Thoughts with wings outspread,—
The splendour of their souls.
Cried one to me," O mortal brother, since thou **lovest too**
With all thy burning breath
The stony hills and salt Corinthian blue
From whose divine dear shore
Apollo led me to the caves of death——"

But charmèd, he forbore.
His voice had sung to measure grave and low
When suddenly his young friend-phantom spoke,
And Shelley's voice rang like a wave of æther
Blazing and breaking on rosy cliffs of air,
And his face was flaming snow, overlushed

By a river of the sun—his long bright hair.
" Inheritor," he sang, " speed thou away
Rushing with Æolus and Boreas, rushing on the
    ancient paths
Scattering the rosy plumage of the new arisen day.

" Go thou to Athens, go to Salonica,
Go thou to Yannina beside the lake,
And cry, ' The vision of the Prophet dead ! '
Cry, ' The Olympians wake ! '
And cry, ' O Towers of Hellas built anew by rhyme,
Star-woven to my Amphionic lyre,
Stand you in steel for ever,
And from your lofty lanterns sweeping the dim hills
    and the nocturnal sea
Pour out the fire of Hellas, the everlasting fire ! ' "

And then to me once more the Elder Shadow :
" Still, brother, Shelley's fancy brims desire :
His soul is so acquainted with great dreams
That even the immane Elysian meadow
Whose flowers are stars and every star a world that
    glides and gleams,
Confines him not—but still he longs to roam
Beyond the quiet spiritual home.
—His soul is so acquainted with great dreams
That man's endeavour
He seeth not near—that broken river
Struggling—to what salt sea ?

" Since man's endeavour flows as a river, how shall it
  turn to the hills again ?
—Burst again all rosy with morning from snow-
  starred mountains of first renown ;
Who to-day shall hear the Achæans shout from the
  trench of the Troyans slain,
Who rebuild in music or memory Sparta's tower or
  Athena's town ?

" Since the Roman intercepted and Rome's dimidiate,
  stoled Byzance,
Shall they hear above their cannon grave, the
  Periclean tune ?
Christ oversang it, chivalry dimmed it, winding on
  Parnès the horns of France,
Islam drowned the echo of echo deep in the night of
  her languid moon."

     *   *   *   *   *

Passionate thus he spake, the wise ghost unforgetful
Of stone and tree, river and shore and plain,
And the good coloured things of Earth the dead see
  not again,
And how man's hope grows weak and his force fretful
With such great hills to gain.
I for an answer pondered deep,
And then I seemed to fall from sleep to sleep,
Watching as through a veil I could not tear
The threads of rose and gold of Shelley's hair.

The gold glowed deeper and the rose burnt red,
And I saw running and rustling at my feet
The rivers of a golden sun that bled
Scarlet, scarlet, scarlet as though wounded
By some celestial archer of the Stars
In the last fight when God's last trump was sounded;
Then the great lake of commingling blood and fire
Burst in a fountain to my window streaming,
To my Cephisian window high and cool,
Over far Salamis and Athens gleaming,
Drowning the sea and city in one deep pool.
And only now old Parnès of the West
And grey Hymettus of the dawn
Rose above the phantom seas
Like Islands of the Blest.

Then a wind came and swept and whirled away,
And the mist left Hymettus broken small
Like a swarm of golden bees.
Gone is the Poet of the magic locks,
And Byron gone ; master of war's [. . . .]
Outflashes white the holy Parthenon
And broad calm streets of Athens of to-day,
And in the barracks the far bugles play,
O listen what they say !

    *   *   *   *   *

Hark, hark the shepherd piping far and near,
The hills are dancing to the Dorian mood.

To-day Arcady is and the white Fear
Naked in sunshine glory still haunts here;
The old dark wood
Invites to prayer—or fountain in the vale.
If not the Cytherean, one more dear
Daphnis shall worship—one more pale,
She too a heroine of a Grecian tale.

   *   *   *   *   *

But if no Pheidias with marble towers
Grace our new Athens, simple, calm and wide,
Carving a group of men to look like flowers
For our new glory's pride.
If songs of gentle Solomos be less
Than that Aeschylean trump of bronze
And if beside Eurotas the lone swans
About the desolation press.

Yet still victorious Hellas, thou hast heard
Those ancient voices thundering to arms,
Thou nation of an older younger day
Thou hast gone forth as with the poet's song.
Surely the spirit of the old oak grove
Rejoiced to hear the cannon round Yannina,
Apollo launched his shaft of terror down
On Salonica. .   .   .   .
  .   .   .   .   .   .

1913

The Old Warship Ablaze

Founder, old battleship ; thy fight is done !
Yonder ablaze like thee now sinks the sun,
Shooting the last grand broadside of his beams
Over thy blackened plates and writhing seams.
Against hard odds thy crew played all their part,
Driving thee deathwards that the foe should smart
Till the guns brake and fire leapt up insane,
And they abandoned thee, to fight again,
Who on thy deck, where flicker the gaunt flames,
Have left so many dead—won such proud names.

Dark flow the waiting waves : one can still see
Thy giant murderer edge sullenly
Eastward among the swelling towers of night.
Canst thou, dying, forget in Hell's despite
Thy freight of fire and blood, the roar and rage
Of waves and guns ?   Thou liest age on age
Tranced like the Princess in her sleepy Thorn,
In that curv'd bay where once the film of morn
Brake azure to thy bugles, skilled to bring
The Afric breeze, who, prompt on honied wing

Silvered the waves and then the olive trees,
And shook like sceptres those stiff companies
The columned palms,—nor till the air was full
Of flash and whisper came the noon-tide lull.
Or that far country's ten-year-buried eves
Or moonlight scattered like a shower of leaves
Dost thou recall ?—Or how on this same deck,
Whose flaming planks blood-boultered tilt to wreck,
The dance went round to music, and how shone
For English grey, black eyes of Lebanon ?

But Eastward and still east the World is thrown
Like a mad hunter seeking dawns unknown
Who plunges deep in sparkless woods of gloom.
Lebanon long hath turned into night's womb
And through her stellèd casements pass new dreams :
Thee too from those last no-more-rival beams
Earth rolleth back. Alone O ship, O flower,
O flame, thou sailest for a moth-weak hour !

They come at last, the bird-soft pattering feet !
Flame high, old ship ; the Fair throng up to greet
Thy splendid doom. See the long spirits, curled
Beside their dead, stand upright free of the world !
And seize the bright shapes loosed from blood-warm sleep,
They, the true ghosts, whose eyes are fixed and deep i

O ship, O fire, O fancy!   A swift roar
Has rent the brow of night.   Thou nevermore
Shalt glide to channel port or Syrian town ;
Light ghosts have danced thee like a plummet down,
And, swift as Fate through skies with storm bestrewn,
Dips out ironical that ship New Moon.

THE END

The Westminster Press
411A Harrow Road
London, W.9

Lightning Source UK Ltd.
Milton Keynes UK
03 March 2011

168587UK00001B/136/P